REINVENTING THE
AUSTIN CITY COUNCIL

In the series **Political Lessons from American Cities,**

edited by Richardson Dilworth

REINVENTING THE
AUSTIN CITY COUNCIL

Ann O'M. Bowman

TEMPLE UNIVERSITY PRESS

Philadelphia • *Rome* • *Tokyo*

TEMPLE UNIVERSITY PRESS
Philadelphia, Pennsylvania 19122
tupress.temple.edu

Library of Congress Cataloging-in-Publication Data

Names: Bowman, Ann O'M., 1948– author.
Title: Reinventing the Austin City Council / Ann O'M. Bowman.
Description: Philadelphia : Temple University Press, 2020. | Series:
  Political lessons from American cities | Includes bibliographical
  references and index. | Summary: "Reinventing the Austin City Council
  explores Austin's reluctance to alter its longstanding electoral system
  of at-large city council districts, its eventual decision to do so, and
  the consequences of this change"— Provided by publisher.
Identifiers: LCCN 2019042799 (print) | LCCN 2019042800 (ebook) | ISBN
  9781439919996 (cloth) | ISBN 9781439920008 (paperback) | ISBN
  9781439920015 (pdf)
Subjects: LCSH: Austin (Tex.). City Council. | Elections—Texas—Austin. |
  Representative government and representation—Texas—Austin. | Austin
  (Tex.)—Politics and government.
Classification: LCC JS567.5 .B68 2020 (print) | LCC JS567.5 (ebook) | DDC
  320.9764/31—dc23
LC record available at https://lccn.loc.gov/2019042799
LC ebook record available at https://lccn.loc.gov/2019042800

Printed in the United States of America

9 8 7 6 5 4 3 2 1

This book is dedicated to the memory of my brother, William Rynbrandt Bowman, who, despite spending more than four decades in Houston and San Antonio, was a fan of Austin.

CONTENTS

PREFACE AND ACKNOWLEDGMENTS

einventing the Austin City Council presents a story of institutional change in Austin, Texas, that is compelling for several reasons, not the least of which is the location: the fast-growing, tech-rich, culturally vibrant capital of Texas. The city is often referred to as the "blueberry in the tomato soup," a sobriquet emblematic of Austin's embrace of left-leaning, progressive policies in a politically conservative state. This book has its genesis in an apparent irony: that this progressive city continued to use an electoral system generally considered nonprogressive long after other large Texas cities had changed theirs. The electoral system in question is one in which candidates for city council compete citywide for seats, and voters can vote for as many candidates as there are seats up for election. This approach, known as an "at-large" system, has been shown to disadvantage the representation of geographically concentrated minority groups, particularly people of color. Other factors affect the outcome of elections, of course, but an at-large structure creates an uneven playing field. After several failed efforts to replace Austin's at-large system, in 2012 voters finally approved a measure establishing a geographically based, single-member district system for electing the city council. *Reinventing the Austin City Council* explores the repeated attempts to change the electoral system, analyzes the successful effort in 2012, and assesses the impact of the new district system since its inception in 2014.

Austin is a place that beckons, hence the continuous surge in new residents and tourists, concomitant development, and favorable media coverage. Many other cities look covetously at Austin, now the nation's eleventh largest city, as a model to emulate. But as Austin has learned, growth and development come with costs as well as benefits. The fruits of growth and development are sweet for some and bitter for others; and these inequitable outcomes present a serious challenge for the city council. The direction the city should take and the policies the council should adopt to address this challenge are at the heart of many debates within the council. Austin remains a city to watch.

This book is intended for multiple audiences including scholars, students, Austinites, and other folks near and far who are interested in cities and, especially, city politics. It does not seek to develop a new theory or engage in definitive empirical tests of hypotheses. But *Reinventing the Austin City Council* is based on theories of representation, and it provides empirical evidence related to political mobilization and institutional change.

Thanks are owed to the many individuals I interviewed in Austin who offered keen insights about the city. These interviews were conducted most frequently in offices but on occasion over breakfast tacos at one of the city's classic dives or while walking along the pathways bordering Lady Bird Lake. Interviewees were promised confidentiality, a research approach intended to maximize candor. Extensive source information was found at the Austin History Center, which is an excellent repository of all things Austin, most particularly, in this case, documents related to the city council. The staff of the center is quite helpful and informed.

The Bush School of Government and Public Service at Texas A&M University provided significant support for this research. Four remarkable Bush School master's degree students served as research assistants: Daniel Tihanyi conducted initial background work and furnished important contextual information, Andrew Garrison spent much of his second year of graduate school on the Austin project and skillfully designed many of the analytics contained in the book, and Joohyung Park and James McKenzie contributed indispensable assistance in the final stages of readying the manuscript for publication. Thanks to all of you for first-rate work. In addition, Austin was a frequent topic of discussion in PSAA 619, a graduate urban policy and management class I taught in the spring semester of 2018. I thank the students enrolled in the class for their discerning observations about Austin. Another group of individuals was quite instrumental in this work: several Bush School graduates residing in Austin offered insightful perspectives on many different issues. I salute your sagacity. Finally, funding from the Hazel Davis and Robert Kennedy Endowed Chair supported frequent research trips to Austin, and I am most grateful.

I thank the three anonymous reviewers for their astute comments and thoughtful recommendations, which have improved this book. Also, feedback from participants on urban politics panels at meetings of the American Political Science Association, the Southern Political Science Association, and the Urban Affairs Association was helpful in the early stages of the research.

Much credit goes to Richardson Dilworth for developing this important book series, *Political Lessons from American Cities*. Thank you, Richard, for the invitation to contribute a book on Austin to the series. The staff at Temple University Press has been excellent to work with from start to finish. Their commitment to publishing work on urban politics is noteworthy. Colleagues, family, and friends, many of whom have heard more about Austin than they probably wanted to, deserve a shout-out for their tolerance and support.

A. O'M. B.

REINVENTING THE
AUSTIN CITY COUNCIL

INTRODUCTION

The Best Place to Live in America?

A
ustin is not the biggest city in Texas, but a case could be made for it being the most interesting large city in the Lone Star State. Although it shares some characteristics with its big-city counterparts—Houston, San Antonio, Dallas, Fort Worth, and El Paso—it is markedly different in many ways.[1] Not only is Austin the capital of Texas; it has proclaimed itself "the live music capital of the world." It embraces a quirky specialness, to wit, the "Keep Austin Weird" promotional campaign. After all, what other city hosts "Spamarama," an occasional event that celebrates the often-mocked canned spiced meat? Where else do hundreds of residents and visitors alike gather along a bridge at sunset to watch more than one million bats take to the sky?

Another difference is the city's plan for the future, a plan that can be loosely summed up as a hope that the benefits of growth will reach all communities in the city.[2] This vision of the future is contested because it coexists with a persistent tension between what urban sociologist Anthony Orum termed "capitalists and democrats," which often takes the form of conflict among developers, environmentalists, and neighborhood groups.[3] In Austin, this conflict is not always resolved in favor of the capitalists/developers. Liberal ideology prevails in Austin, a community that is receptive to progressive ideas and approaches. In addition, Austin's economy is far less dependent on the energy industry that predominates in other parts of the state. Instead, Austin has been said to exemplify Richard Florida's conception of a creative city, one in which technology is a major component of the local economy, and arts and cultural activity are essential elements.[4] Austin scores high on measures of venture capital investment and start-up formation; it leads other large cities in the state in the requisite education and skills of a creative city workforce.[5] Moreover, city government was an early investor in the local art and music scene. Together, these factors cause Austin to stand out amid other big cities in Texas. And it stands out beyond its Lone Star state counterparts: in 2017 and 2018, *U.S. News & World Report* named Austin as the best place to live in America, based on quality of life, job prospects, and affordability.[6]

Any one of these features could be a subject worthy of research, but it is another significant difference that is the focus of this book: until 2014, Austin elected its entire city council at large. In other words, candidates for the governing body competed in citywide elections and the Austin electorate could vote for every seat. This type of electoral system generates numerous consequences, and it does not fit the profile of Austin as a progressive city.

City councils are worthy of study in that they are the "custodians of place," to borrow a phrase used by urban policy scholars Paul Lewis and Max Nieman.[7] The council's decisions affect the city today and chart the city's path to the future. The method of the council's selection influences who is elected, whose interests are represented, and ergo, what decisions are made. Austin's resistance to changing its electoral system, its eventual decision to do so, and the consequences of the new district-based system make for a compelling story.

Austin: A Blueberry in the Tomato Soup

Among the six biggest cities in Texas, Austin is the most liberal in terms of ideology, giving a greater share of its vote to recent Democratic presidential candidates.[8] The liberal-leaning city is often at odds with the conservative political leadership of the state and has been called "a blue island in a sea of red," or, more evocatively, "a blueberry in the tomato soup."[9] This ideological divergence has widened as the conservatism of the legislature has increased, and as a result Austin is often singled out for special attention from the legislature. A dispute between developers and environmentalists more than twenty-five years ago is illustrative. In 1992, Austin's voters approved Save Our Springs, an initiative intended to regulate the development of land and preserve the quality of water in local watersheds. The development community opposed the new ordinance, hired a lobbyist, and turned to the state legislature for relief. The lobbyist convinced legislators that developers should be grandfathered in under the rules that existed at the time they purchased the land rather than being forced to comply with new regulations put in place subsequently by Save Our Springs.[10] The legislature passed an anti–Save Our Springs bill in 1993, but it was vetoed by Democratic governor Ann Richards. The following session, the bill to overturn Austin's ordinance was passed once again, and, this time, it was signed by Republican governor George W. Bush. The developers' lobbyist rejoiced, commenting hyperbolically that "the legislature has burned Austin to the ground."[11]

The efforts to burn continue. In the 2017 legislative session, proposals to preempt Austin's ban on single-use plastic bags, its regulations for ride-hailing companies such as Uber and Lyft, its regulations on short-term residential rentals, its tree protection ordinances, and its policies that make Austin a sanctuary-like city were introduced. *Texas Monthly* summed up the tense relationship between the capital city and the legislature in this way: "In recent years, the Texas Legislature has passed laws restricting what regulations cities can pass—especially if they originate in Austin."[12] For a blue city like Austin, crafting policy solutions that are responsive to citizen preferences, without raising the ire of a conservative legislature, is a continual challenge.

The Electoral Difference and Contextual Conditions

Beyond its rocky relationship with state government, Austin provides an important political lesson about representation in a fast-changing urban environment. As noted above, until 2014, Austin was the largest city in the country to operate with a city council elected entirely at large, an electoral system that typically has the effect of reducing representation of minority groups. One consequence of the at-large structure was that, according to the city's demographer, "70 percent of those elected to the council come from areas of town where 35 percent of the population lives, and all council members live within three to four miles of each other."[13] Hardly the electoral outcome one would expect in a city that celebrates its liberalism and forward-thinking nature. Huge swaths of the nearly three hundred square mile city had experienced limited to no representation for many decades. And, although, since the 1980s, the city council had regularly included an African American and a Hispanic among its membership, many observers questioned whether city government was sufficiently responsive to the interests of racial and ethnic minorities.[14]

Austin's continued reliance on an electoral system that can produce disproportionate and discriminatory electoral outcomes is at odds with a city that embraces a progressive ethos. Other big Texas cities, most of them with council-manager forms of government as in Austin, had already switched to a geographic-based district system or a mixed district/at-large structure as far back as the 1970s. What explains the apparent anomaly in Austin?

In considering an answer to this question, several contextual conditions loom large: Austin's status as a leading "creative city," the ongoing strains among the development community, local environmentalists, and neighborhoods, and the contested vision of Austin's future held by city leaders both inside and outside of city government. These contextual conditions intersect regularly when it comes to city policy making.

Austin's Status as a Leading Creative City

In his 2002 book, *The Rise of the Creative Class*, Richard Florida theorized that the postindustrial economy is increasingly driven by what he calls the "creative class," defined as knowledge-based professionals in science and engineering, health care, and finance as well as "people in design, education, arts, music and entertainment, whose economic function is to create new ideas, new technology and/or creative content."[15] Cities (or more accurately, metropolitan areas) that attract the creative class will be the successful entrepreneurial cities of the twenty-first century. According to Florida, three characteristics are necessary for a city to attract and retain the creative class: talent (a highly talented, educated, and skilled population), tolerance (a diverse community with a "live and let live" ethos), and technology (the technological infrastructure necessary to fuel an entrepreneurial culture).

Austin, based on the metrics used in Florida's creativity index, was a prototypical creative city.[16] Subsequent criticism of Florida's argument and measures notwithstanding,[17] the book created a stir in Austin as the city proclaimed its designation at or near the top of the list, depending on the data year. Florida relates the story of a Carnegie-Mellon University graduate who spurned high-tech job offers in Pittsburgh to take a position in Austin. His important considerations when making the decision included liking the people in the software company and the work he would be doing, but the determinative factor was that the company was located in Austin, a city that offered the kind of lifestyle he was seeking.[18]

The desirability of Austin was not confined to recent college graduates in the high-tech field. Others in the creative class found Austin beckoning, and, as a result, the city's population and job base have increased rapidly and substantially. But this high rate of growth and development has produced several negative externalities: rapid escalation in the cost of housing, intensification of traffic congestion, increased pollution and the destruction of natural resources, a growing sense that the quality of life has diminished, and the emergence of tension between the high-salaried high-tech workers and the low-salaried local artists.[19] Florida eventually acknowledged some of the downsides for creative cities, noting, for one, that:

On close inspection, talent clustering (in creative cities) provides little in the way of trickle-down benefits. Its benefits flow disproportionately to more highly-skilled knowledge, professional and creative workers whose higher wages and salaries are more than sufficient to cover more expensive housing in these locations. While less-skilled service and blue-collar workers also earn more money in knowledge-based metros, those gains disappear once their higher housing costs are taken into account.[20]

Being a creative city is not the unalloyed good that it was initially perceived to be. In fact, success at being a creative city appears to generate its own set of problems, many that are within the purview of city government to resolve. Consider the perspective of Javier Auyero, a sociologist who led an ethnographic study of Austin, which he referred to as "a thriving, rapidly growing, highly unequal, and segregated technopolis."[21] In theory, a geographically based city council should be more attuned to addressing these sorts of concerns than an at-large council would be.

Developers, Environmentalists, and Neighborhoods

Some issues in Austin pit adherents of what sociologist Harvey Molotch called "the growth machine" against what could be termed "quality-of-life enthusiasts."[22] In Austin, the issue that unites quality-of-life advocates is the maintenance of the environment, that is, the city's natural attributes and its neighborhood scale. These types of clashes occur in communities throughout the United States, but what makes Austin remarkable is that environmentalists and neighborhood groups, through their fervor, persistence, and numbers, have become key players in local planning and policy-making processes. Their impact is evident, for instance, in the 1979 Austin Tomorrow Comprehensive Plan, which "largely reflected the aspirations of those Austin citizens concerned about the destructive effects of continued urbanization on their neighborhoods and natural environment."[23]

Over the past fifty years, many Austin City Council candidates have run on green platforms, and, if elected, they set about building coalitions with other council members to form a voting bloc. As a result, environmental perspectives have been brought to bear on numerous issues confronting city leaders. Furthermore, the city created an Environmental Commission to "act in an advisory capacity on all projects and programs which affect the quality of life for the citizens of Austin."[24] Neighborhood groups and homeowners' associations abound in Austin, many of which are affiliated with the Austin Neighborhoods Council, an umbrella organization that holds much sway in city politics. Their policy preferences at times—but not always—align with the views of the environmental community.

However, it would be a mistake to overlook the influence of the business community, and especially development interests, in Austin. The growth of a prosperous city is their top priority, and, although they are not oblivious to environmental concerns and neighborhood impacts, these factors are not necessarily paramount. All three interests—environmental groups, neighborhood associations, and the development community—often support council candidates through public endorsements and campaign funding. Their involvement does not end there; they regularly lobby council members on issues that come before the governing body.

Although jockeying among these interests persists, the Austin way is to attempt to find common ground. The model for this approach is the Smart Growth Initiative (SGI) of the late 1990s, led by an Austin mayor who had a reputation as a mediator and was later elected to the state senate. Voters approved a package of $712 million in bond issues for city improvements in support of SGI. The city began developing several empty city-owned blocks offering tax abatements and fee waivers to private developers who selected in-town building sites rather than raw land on the outskirts of the city.[25]

Over time, SGI has led to the densification of downtown Austin with the construction of sleek office towers and high-rise residences as well as mixed-use developments. As anticipated, it has reduced pressure for the development of pristine land on the city's edges. One observer commented, "Smart Growth meant that Austin could grow its economy best by preserving that which attracted people to Austin: its environment."[26] But over time, SGI spurred gentrification of close-in East Austin neighborhoods, areas with proportionately large numbers of African Americans and Hispanics. Longtime residents and businesses have been displaced, a phenomenon the city council was slow to address. Balancing the interests of environmentalists, neighborhood activists, and developers to find common ground is not an easy task.

The Contested Vision of Austin's Future

Mayors and city council members typically have a sense of where their city fits among other cities. Moreover, they often have a vision of what the city could become, that is, an aspiration for the future. In pursuit of that vision, the city council often mobilizes public capital, investing its resources in desired economic development projects and supporting causes and events that promote the city.[27] Seldom is Austin mentioned among the United States' so-called world cities, such as New York, Los Angeles, and Chicago. Some Austin leaders would like to see their city become part of that top tier of U.S. cities.

In pursuit of this vision, in 2015, one of Austin's assistant city managers dispatched his staff to study whether Austin would be well served by constructing a sports stadium to attract a professional team to the city. After all, he reasoned, major cities in the United States are home to professional sports teams, and, to be a big-league city, you need a stadium. The staff found that the consensus among sports economists was that public investment in sports stadiums rarely pays off.[28] Professional sporting events are one more competitor for the local entertainment dollar; they typically do not stimulate additional spending but instead move existing spending around. The stadium idea was shelved, only to reemerge more forcefully in 2018 when the city council voted 7–4 to approve a deal for a privately financed major league soccer stadium on city-owned land, with the expectation of attracting a franchise relocating from Columbus, Ohio. The goal of pushing the city onto a higher plane among the pantheon of great U.S. cities remains among some local leaders but, at the same time, others lament the passing of the quirky Austin. Still others have a different vision, one in which Austin strengthens its commitment to social justice and equity to become a place where the voices of the less fortunate are heard and responded to.

One local entertainment event that has put Austin on the national stage is South by Southwest (SXSW). It began as a local music festival that, in its first year (1987), attracted seven hundred people who paid $10 for a wristband giving them access to all of the venues. Now, the ten-day event features, in addition to music, film and interactive media and attracts more than eighty thousand registrants from across the country, with an individual all-access festival ticket costing between $1,150 and $1,650. Many locals grumble that the success of the event has priced them out of attendance. As suggested above, they are not alone in believing that the city is moving along the wrong path.

In March 2016, the publication *Texas Monthly* featured a lengthy discussion that compared laid-back "old Austin" with tech-savvy, design-conscious "new Austin."[29] One question recurred throughout the piece: "Has Austin lost its soul?" As an unsuccessful candidate for the city council in 2014 commented, "We have gotten caught up in feeding a growth industry. It's like we're on one of those hamster wheels and we're afraid to stop."[30] What does Austin want to be? Where does it fit? Is what made Austin uniquely Austin being sacrificed amid a quest to move to a higher tier of cities? Ultimately, what kind of vision will prevail?[31]

The Road Ahead

The three contextual conditions discussed above set the stage for the consideration of a conundrum: Why did a progressive city retain a decidedly nonprogressive electoral system long after other big cities in the state had replaced their at-large systems? For forty years, repeated proposals to adopt a more progressive geographically based system for electing council members were defeated by Austin voters. Then, in 2012, voters approved a ballot measure to elect city council members from ten geographic districts, with only the mayor being elected citywide. Two puzzles motivate the research in *Reinventing the Austin City Council*: one is the explanation for the long delay and the eventual adoption of a district system; the other is the impact of the new districts on the operations and outputs of the council and on the residents of Austin.

For source material, this case study relies on documents available at the Austin History Center, news media accounts, prior studies conducted by social scientists, and semistructured interviews with numerous Austinites, as city residents are called. Among those interviewed were longtime observers of Austin politics, leaders of local civic groups, community activists, local political consultants, and current and former elected officials and city staff.

The book proceeds in this manner. In Chapter 1, the focus is on how Austin became the city it is today by looking at the evolution of its government, particularly the city council. Chapter 2 addresses Austin's system of representation, and its repeated consideration—and voter rejection—of geographic districts, leading up to voter approval in 2012. In Chapter 3, the focus shifts to consequences, what the change in the electoral system has meant for the city. The book concludes with a thematic summary and a look ahead.

HOW AUSTIN BECAME THE CITY IT IS TODAY . . . AND WHAT THE CITY COUNCIL HAD TO DO WITH IT

I n 1839, the town of Waterloo, soon to be renamed Austin, became the capital of the Republic of Texas. When it was chosen as the capital, the president of the young republic, Sam Houston, remarked that Austin was the "most unfortunate site upon earth for the seat of government."[1] Upon the admission of Texas to the union in 1846, Austin, unfortunate or not, maintained its status as capital of the new state. When Austin's population was first officially taken four years later, 629 hardy individuals were counted. They had to be hardy because by all accounts, life in the newly constituted city was difficult.[2] The area was a wilderness, and the white settlers, Native Americans, and Mexicans fought over ownership of the land. The settlers were successful in displacing both groups, and, by the time of the 1860 census, the population had grown to 3,494, a more than 400 percent increase during the decade. Growth was a persistent feature of the Texas capital. Over the ensuing decades, Austin's population growth rate dropped below 20 percent only once, from 1910 to 1920 when it grew by 16.8 percent.

This chapter begins with a brief look at Austin, particularly its growth in both population and land area and its appeal as a community. From there, the focus shifts to a broad look at city councils: what they do and how they have been reformed. To put the Austin case in perspective, the chapter presents a summary of the research that has been conducted on electoral systems, more specifically, the at-large and geographic district systems. Of particular interest is answering the question of how the use of one or the other affects the council's policies and performance and the representation of the community. The last section of the chapter returns the focus to Austin to trace the evolution of city government from its beginning in the mid-nineteenth century to the current period.

Changes and Comparisons

In 1950, Austin was the seventy-third largest city in the United States in terms of population and it occupied 32.1 square miles of territory. Since then both the population and the land area of the city have exploded. As of 2018, Austin's population size made it the nation's eleventh largest city. In terms of geography, the core or central part of the city includes the downtown area and the University of Texas campus. From there, the city can be divided into South Austin (south of Lady Bird Lake), East Austin (the area of the city lying east of Interstate 35), North Austin (often said to start near Forty-Fifth Street), and West Austin (generally the area west of the Mopac Expressway).

Due to the state's permissive annexation laws, the city's land area has increased as well, now covering three hundred square miles.[3] Recent annexations have pushed the city's limits beyond Travis County into the bordering county to the north, Williamson, and to the south, Hays County. Figure 1.1 tracks the patterns in the rates of growth for each decade from 1900 to 2010 for Austin's population and land area. As is readily apparent, Austin has had many decades in which population growth exceeded 40 percent as well as several spikes in land area, most notably during the 1980s. The 20 percent growth in population and the 18 percent increase in land area during the first decade of the twenty-first century, which would be notable in most large cities, are fairly modest by Austin standards.

Austin differs from other large cities in Texas on many demographic and socioeconomic indicators. Table 1.1 compares Austin, whose 2017 population estimate by the Census Bureau was 950,715, with the other five Texas cities that have populations of a half million or more: Houston (2,312,717), San Antonio (1,511,946), Dallas (1,341,075), Fort Worth (874,168), and El Paso (683,577).[4] The points of comparison are aspects of population growth, racial diversity, education levels, home values, and characteristics of the labor force.

As is evident from the data in the table, Austin is growing at a higher rate, has a population that is less racially and ethnically diverse, and has higher levels of education than other big cities in the state. The average value of housing is greater, proportionately more women participate in the labor force, and a higher share of workers is employed in Richard Florida's "creative city" occupations.[5] These features coalesce to produce a city that is fairly atypical of other jurisdictions in the state. In fact, some Austinites

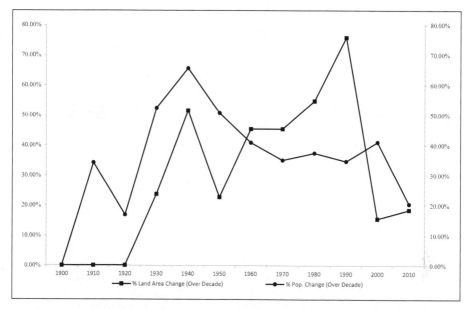

Figure 1.1. Austin's population and land area changes by decade, 1900–2010.
(Sources: Census of Population and Housing, various dates; City of Austin, accessed March 7, 2018, available at http://www.austintexas.gov//page/district-demographics.)

tend to see their community as more akin to a San Francisco, Boston, or San Jose than to their Texas counterparts. There is active resistance in many corners to the notion that Austin should endeavor to become another Houston or Dallas; the desire to preserve the lifestyle that is uniquely Austin is held dearly by many local residents. In terms of politics, urban Texas tends to be less conservative than rural Texas, but the data displayed in Table 1.2 suggest that Austin stands out among its big-city brethren for its liberal ideology and partisan proclivities.

It is not difficult to discern why Austin is so celebrated by longtime residents and recent arrivals alike. The natural beauty of the Texas hill country, the vibrant arts and cultural scene, the ubiquitous funky food trucks that coexist with upscale restaurants, and the presence of the University of Texas at Austin are but a few of the area's attractions. Geographer Joshua Long, author of *Weird City: Sense of Place and Creative Resistance in Austin, Texas*, averred that an "Austin exceptionalism" exists, a sense that Austinites "live in a vortex of perpetual cool."[6] This assessment has more than a modicum of truth to it. In a 2017 poll, three-quarters of residents surveyed used these words to describe Austin: musical, creative, young, educated, entrepreneurial, liberal, innovative, and healthy.[7] But these positive images mask an ever-present tension over quality-of-life issues. To what should this cool city as-

TABLE 1.1. SELECTED FEATURES OF THE SIX LARGEST CITIES IN TEXAS

City	Population change (%) 2010–2017	White alone, not Hispanic or Latino (%), 2012–2016	Bachelor's degree or higher, persons age 25+ (%) 2012–2016	Median value ($) owner-occupied housing units, 2012–2016	Women in the labor force (%), 2012–2016	Share of labor force in "creative city" occupations (%), 2016*
Austin	18.5	48.9	47.7	257,800	76.1	49.65
Dallas	12.0	29.2	31.0	142,600	70.1	34.75
El Paso	5.5	14.0	23.6	119,300	66.4	35.38
Fort Worth	17.3	40.7	27.6	131,100	69.5	34.81
Houston	10.4	25.1	31.2	140,300	70.1	36.65
San Antonio	13.9	25.5	25.2	121,100	70.3	34.55

Source: U.S. Census Bureau, American Fact Finder, 2017 Population Estimates; 2012–2016 American Community Survey 5-Year Estimates; various tables, accessed May 25, 2018, available at https://factfinder.census.gov/faces/nav/jsf/pages/index.xhtml.

* Creative city occupations include all workers in the following occupational classifications: management, business, and finance; computer science and mathematics; architecture and engineering; life, physical, and social sciences; arts, design, entertainment, sports, and media; health care; law; and education, training, and library.

TABLE 1.2. LARGE TEXAS CITIES: CITIZEN IDEOLOGY AND VOTE CHOICE

City	Austin	Dallas	El Paso	Fort Worth	Houston	San Antonio
Citizen policy preferences	−0.53	−0.23	−0.07	0	−0.17	−0.01
City vote for Obama, 2008	70.7%	64.7%	65.4%	54.8%	61.7%	56.2%

Sources: Data from Chris Tausanovitch and Christopher Warshaw, "Representation in Municipal Government," *American Political Science Review* 108, no. 3 (2014): 605–664; American Ideology Project, accessed April 29, 2018, available at http://www.americanideologyproject.com/.

Note: The more negative the preference value, the more liberal the citizenry.

pire? The city's comprehensive plan, *Imagine Austin*, ratchets it up a notch with this grand vision statement: "Austin is a beacon of sustainability, social equity, and economic opportunity; where diversity and creativity are celebrated; where community needs and values are recognized; where leadership comes from its citizens, and where the necessities of life are affordable and accessible to all."[8] This is a prodigious vision and the responsibility for pursuing it lies at the feet of the Austin City Council.

City Councils: Roles, Representation, and Reform

City councils are complex institutions, and, perhaps because of that, they are fascinating to observe and study. First of all, consider their locus. City council members make policy not from the lofty perch of a state capital or

Washington, DC, but instead at city hall in the community in which they live. In other words, they serve their hometown constituents from their hometown. As a result, these governing bodies are very much about place. And this locus leads to one of the most notable characteristics of a city council: its accessibility to the public it serves. Also, when city councils make policy they do so in a web of relationships: vertically with the state and federal governments, horizontally with other local governments in their region. These other jurisdictions have both a direct and an indirect impact on the policy a city adopts. Moreover, webs of relationships exist with nongovernmental entities as well, including numerous connections to nonprofit organizations and business firms. Consequently, although a city government enjoys a considerable level of authority and discretion within its territorial limits, it is not immune to the decisions and actions of these other entities.

When political scientists Heinz Eulau and Kenneth Prewitt undertook their exhaustive study of eighty-two city councils in the San Francisco Bay region, their intent was to examine "how the distance . . . between the representatives of the people and the represented can be minimized so that the values of democracy can be maximized."[9] Although their study was conducted in the mid-1960s, fifty-plus years later, the research question motivating *Labyrinths of Democracy* is still relevant. And as we shall see, it has particular relevance in Austin.

The Eulau and Prewitt research shone a bright light on the behavior of city councils, in particular "the linkage between the governing few and the many who are governed."[10] They found that councils developed their own governing styles and practices and that the size of the council (more so than the size of the city) exercised a strong influence on council dynamics. Some councils functioned more cohesively, others were more fractious and fragmented. The degree of conflict in council decision-making varied; behaviors common to legislative settings such as bargaining and reciprocity, compromise, and coalition formation occurred at times.

One of the defining characteristics of members of legislative bodies in a representative democracy is their role orientation. Do they consider themselves to be delegates of their constituents and consequently act in accordance with constituent preferences? Or, do they see themselves as trustees of the public's interest, and, as a result, take actions they believe are best for the city, even if these actions conflict with majority preferences? For the council members interviewed for *Labyrinths of Democracy*, the role orientation was relatively clear: 60 percent of council interviewees described themselves as trustees, only 18 percent identified as delegates. The remaining 22 percent either could not choose between the orientations or said that they adjusted their orientation to fit the circumstances of a certain issue.[11]

National surveys of city council members at different points in time suggest a continuing tension over the nature of representation and role orientations. Should a council member rely on his or her own sense of what is best for the community or is it more appropriate for a council member to act as the delegate of constituents and follow their dictates? After all, candidates for city council often espouse policy positions during the campaign; they may interpret their election as a mandate to pursue those policies. But once in office, elected officials find themselves surrounded by a wide range of groups and constituents whose perspectives may differ. Likewise, city staff may provide council members with additional information about an issue thereby further complicating council decision-making. Over time, each council member develops a calculus for decision-making, often subject to the variability of particular issues. And, of course, individual council member votes are aggregated so, ceteris paribus, a single council member's impact can be modest. Clearly, decision-making by a city council can be fraught with complexity and carries consequences both intended and unforeseen.

Elections, and, in particular, competitive elections, are considered the fundamental mechanisms connecting the government to the public.[12] Most of the cities included in the San Francisco Bay area study utilized an at-large system for electing city council members, as did Austin for more than one hundred years. In an at-large election, candidates compete citywide and those receiving the most votes win the available seats. For example, if there are five seats up for election, then the top five vote getters win those seats. Incumbents and challengers alike compete in what could be termed an organized free-for-all. Each voter can vote for as many candidates as there are available seats. Five seats means that a voter can vote for five different candidates.

The at-large electoral system was a central feature in a package of proposals intended to reform city government. These reforms were developed at the turn of the twentieth century by organizations such as the National Municipal League, and they were promoted as a way to counteract the power of political machines that operated in some cities, especially older cities in the Northeast and Midwest. Political parties were important as mobilizing forces, and, within them, political bosses often emerged to exert inordinate power over local politics—and city government.[13] Exemplifying the maxim, "To the victor goes the spoils," machine supporters won city jobs and contracts for services, opponents did not. Urban reformers contended that these local political machines were corrupt and inefficient, and, as a solution, they argued for a city government run by experts imbued with a more business-like approach. One of the foundations of political machines was the use of geographically based districts or wards—essentially, a collection of neighborhoods—from which city council members or aldermen were elected. At the ward level, subordinates of the political boss served as conduits between the neighborhoods and the machine. Replacing wards with at-large elections was expected to break this connection and, reformers argued, imbue city council members with a citywide perspective. In addition to an at-large system, reformers advocated the use of nonpartisan elections, off-cycle elections, short ballots, civil service systems, and a change in the form of city government.[14]

Initially, reformers pinned their hopes on the commission form of government; eventually, they settled on the council-manager form as the ideal structure to bring about the expertise and professionalism they sought. Local business leaders and groups such as chambers of commerce often became actively involved in the reform movement in their cities. Moreover, there was a class basis to support or opposition to reform. When reforms to city charters were put before voters, middle-class voters were more likely to favor them and working-class voters were more likely to reject them.[15] Reformers found success in many cities, particularly cities in the South and West, and eventually at-large electoral systems became standard in most U.S. cities.

At-Large and District Electoral Systems: Lessons from Research

"What difference does it make if city council members are elected at-large, or by geographically defined districts or wards?"[16] This was the question posed by political scientists Peggy Heilig and Robert Mundt in their 1984 book, *Your Voice at City Hall*. They answered their own question:

> Like most rules, electoral procedures are not neutral. At-large systems favor the electoral chances of certain groups of urban dwellers; theoretically, at least, district elections should favor other groups, and changes from at-large to district systems should lead to new patterns of power and benefit distribution.[17]

This is precisely why it matters: electoral systems advantage some groups and disadvantage others. They affect election outcomes and, by extension, the policy decisions and operational practices of city government. The central concern is the underrepresentation of racial and ethnic minority groups, with underrepresentation typically measured as the proportion of seats held by minorities compared to their proportion in the population. The underlying concept is "descriptive representation": the ability of a group to elect one of its own to office. This differs from "substantive representation," whereby an elected official pursues policies reflective of the interests of the group.[18] In theory and in practice, descriptive representation should yield some degree of substantive representation.

The earliest research on electoral systems in U.S. cities found that African Americans were less likely to be elected to city councils in an at-large system than they were in a single-member district system in which residents vote only in the council race in their district.[19] The explanation for this outcome was summarized by political scientists Richard Engstrom and Michael McDonald in this way:

> Given that racially polarized voting patterns are not uncommon in American cities and that blacks are a minority which is usually concentrated within heavily segregated areas of a city, it has often been asserted that black candidates are far more likely to be elected to city councils through single-member district (or ward) electoral systems than through at-large arrangements.[20]

Although some researchers asserted that socioeconomic factors were more important in electing blacks to city councils than the type of electoral system used in a city,[21] the weight of the evidence from the 1960s and 1970s says otherwise.[22] Studies that varied in terms of the number of cities analyzed and the types and measurement of variables included in the statistical models arrived at a similar conclusion: "In comparison with single-member districts, at-large elections seriously reduce the level of black representation."[23]

As the discussion above indicates, the use of different electoral systems has significant consequences for cities . . . and for representation more specifically. After passage of the federal Voting Rights Act of 1965, litigation became a viable mechanism for forcing city governments to enact changes in their electoral systems to correct for the underrepresentation of racial and ethnic minorities on local governing boards. One of the most significant corrective changes has been a move from at-large elections to district elections for city council. More research has followed and our understanding of the impact of electoral systems has broadened.

Cities That Switched Their Electoral Systems

Your Voice at City Hall uses a series of before and after tests to compare eleven cities that had changed their electoral systems from at-large to districts.[24] As expected, switching to districts resulted in more minority candidates competing for council seats and achieving a higher level of success in winning council seats than before the change. However, even with these increases, minority composition on the council did not necessarily equal their proportion in the city itself. Furthermore, the use of districts, on average, did not necessarily produce socioeconomic variation on the council nor reduce significantly the cost of winning a seat. Additionally, although districts were expected to increase the likelihood that council members would see themselves as delegates rather than trustees, the affluence of a district conditioned the relationship. In other words, council members from upper-income districts saw themselves as trustees while their counterparts elected from poor districts "gave descriptions of the councilmanic role infused with a sense of personal responsibility for their constituents and for their part of the city."[25]

Some of the hypothesized impacts of the switch to district-based councils were realized, others were not. In the short term, the introduction of districts stimulated the creation of discernible voting coalitions on the several councils, particularly those in which the previously underrepresented groups were cohesive.[26] With regard to the allocation of city services, although the advent of district seats did not produce a significant shift, the change did seem to affect the geographic location of new city facilities. An expected increase in the amount of conflict in a district-based council was not readily apparent; instead conflict appeared to be related to whether district council members brought new interests and issues to the council agenda. Nor did districts generate extensive policy benefits for previously underrepresented constituencies.

Early research focused on the impact of electoral systems on the representation of African Americans; later research has looked at other racial and ethnic minorities, especially Hispanics. An analysis of the electoral success of Mexican Americans in Texas cities found that electoral systems had limited impact; rather the size of the Mexican American population was the primary explanation.[27] Still, in cities in which the Mexican American population proportion was low, district systems did increase the representation of Mexican Americans on the city council. After cities changed their electoral systems, more Mexican Americans ran for and won city council seats. Once elected, these district council members tended to have more of a neighborhood orientation than at-large council members did; Mexican American council members had a strong constituency service focus. Notably, some substantive policy effects emerged as a result of having more ethnic minorities on city councils.

The Views of City Council Members

Another way to gauge the impact of electoral systems is to compare city council members themselves. A nationwide survey of almost one thousand council members conducted by political scientists Susan Welch and Timothy Bledsoe in the 1980s offered several points of departure regarding the characteristics, attitudes, and behaviors of council members. For example, at-large members tended to be wealthier and more highly educated than council members elected from districts.[28] Correspondingly, the use of districts created opportunities for the election of individuals with lower incomes and less education. Not surprisingly, council members' perspectives varied. The researchers found that "at-large members are more likely to see the city as a whole as their constituency, and those elected from districts to see the neighborhood as theirs."[29] At-large council members also differed from district members in terms of their relationships with constituents. Council members elected at-large reported devoting less time to dealing with inquiries and requests from individual residents, instead directing more of their attention to citywide issues and business constituencies.

District council members perceived more conflict on the council than at-large council members did; similarly, there was less unanimity in council decisions on district councils. When queried about nine issues that could cause conflict on the council, both at-large and district council members listed the same three issues in the same rank order: prodevelopment versus antidevelopment, tax-cutters versus opponents, and business versus neighborhoods. However, the fourth most prevalent conflict for district council members involved allocational decisions, or what was termed "one area vs. another."[30] But, for at-large council members, the issue of geographic rivalries landed at the bottom of their list of council conflicts. In an effort to determine whether citizens' level of efficacy varied between at-large and district systems, Welch and Bledsoe linked their data to earlier citizen surveys. They found differing results for blacks and whites. For black residents, living in a city with district elections significantly increased feelings of political efficacy; for whites, there was no difference in efficaciousness between the electoral systems.[31]

Recent Research on Electoral Systems

Although nearly half of U.S. cities with populations of twenty-five hundred or more use an at-large method for electing their council members, the popularity of the method declines as population size increases. Among large cities (defined as those with populations of two hundred thousand or more), 49 percent of them use districts exclusively, 38 percent operate with a combination of district and at-large, and 13 percent use at-large elections.[32] The data also confirm previous studies showing that, compared to council members elected citywide, council members elected from districts are more likely to be from racial and ethnic minority groups. District council members also tend to be slightly younger, on average, than their at-large counterparts. When it comes to gender, the type of electoral system appears to make no difference in election outcomes. Notably, some of these effects are greater in cities with a council-manager form of government as opposed to mayor-council cities. But, and this goes to the heart of the matter in Austin, district elections are less common in council-manager cities than in mayor-council cities.

Our understanding of the impact of electoral systems on representation continues to evolve and deepen. For example, research by political scientists Zoltan Hajnal and Jessica Trounstine shows that at-large electoral systems persist in impeding the election of African Americans to city councils.[33] But their findings contain an important clarification, the timing of local elections also has an impact. Elections that are held off-cycle from elections held in November of even-numbered years result in lower voter turnout, which further decreases the likelihood that African American city council candidates will be successful. As they state, "Moving from at-large to district elections and changing the dates of local elections to coincide with the dates of national elections would increase the proportion of blacks on city councils by a little over 6%."[34] Their data indicate that Hispanics and Asians would not benefit as greatly from such changes, which they attribute to lower levels of residential segregation and less racially polarized voting for these groups. For Hispanics and Asians, increases in turnout hold much promise of greater electoral success.

When gender is taken into account, electoral systems differentially affect blacks and Hispanics.[35] An analysis of more than seven thousand cities showed that, although district systems can increase diversity on the council, the effect is most impactful for African American males; for African American women and for Hispanics, the electoral system is of negligible importance. White women typically tend to fare better in at-large systems, but it is also clear that a larger council is an important factor in their electoral success.

After years of research on the question of at-large and district electoral systems, there can be no equivocation: electoral systems affect the outcome of elections. The effect may vary in its magnitude from one city to another, and it may not be the same for all underrepresented groups, but electoral systems have an impact on who wins and who loses. Furthermore, election outcomes affect the policy responsiveness of local governments.[36] After all, as Eulau and Prewitt concluded nearly a half century ago, "the problem of the distance between governors and governed will continue to be high on the agenda of theorizing about democracy."[37]

The Evolution of City Government in Austin

Electing city council members from districts might be new to contemporary Austin, but it was actually quite common in early Austin. When the city was incorporated in late December 1839, its charter established a governmental structure consisting of "one Mayor and eight Alderman, who shall constitute the City Council; one Recorder, one treasurer, one city Marshal."[38] The first city election took place in January 1840, and, after this election, the city was divided into eight geographically separate wards or districts. For the ensuing sixty years, although the mayor was elected at-large, city council members were almost always elected from wards. Granted, there were anomalies during that period such as early in the Reconstruction Era following the Civil War when the governor of Texas appointed Austin's mayor and aldermen.[39] But for the most part, Austin's system of representation on the city council was district-based during the nineteenth century.

As it is now, the charter was the foundation of city government, spelling out the powers and responsibilities of the city council. However, unlike the present day, during the first several decades of Austin's existence, the state legislature effectively controlled the charter, proposing amendments and revising various provisions. The city's scope of operations was limited to the functions laid out in the charter, such as public safety, sanitation, street maintenance, and taxation. The council's power to pass ordinances was similarly constrained by the charter. If the charter did not authorize council action to, for example, issue bonds for new construction or regulate gambling establishments, then the council could not do so. Over time, the city's scope expanded as the legislature authorized additional functions, but it was not until the adoption of a home rule amendment to the state constitution in 1912 that Texas city governments gained inherent powers, that is, a degree of self-governing authority.

Revisions to Austin's charter led to several changes in the number of wards and council members. In 1873, the number of wards was increased to ten; in 1890, the creation of another ward brought the total to eleven. The size of the council doubled for a time when a charter change provided for the election of two aldermen from each district.[40] Amid these structural changes, ward politicians continued to prevail, and, in many instances, political parties became involved in city elections, most typically in nominating and promoting slates of candidates.[41] As in many other cities, ward leaders tended to be individuals such as local shopkeepers, grocers, and saloon operators— occupations that brought them into regular contact with the public. Among the most successful of them in Austin was Andrew Zilker, a self-made businessman who had arrived in Austin from the Midwest virtually penniless at age eighteen.[42] One of Zilker's talents was identifying individuals to run for city council on slates he assembled and funded. He served on the council for a short period but more important was the political organization he created that would continue to be influential into the 1930s.[43]

Reform Comes to Austin

In the 1890s, Austin's politics began to shift. Businessmen and civic leaders were emerging as a potential countervailing force in local politics, challenging the dominance of ward politicians. As was occurring in other cities around this time, this new business elite sought a restructuring of city government. Not coincidentally, in 1897, the legislature called for revision of Austin's charter and supported provisions that would significantly restructure the city council. One provision would decrease the number of wards from eleven to seven and another would institute an at-large vote for aldermen from each ward. Recognizing that these proposals, if approved, would disrupt the city's political system, aldermen petitioned the legislature for a popular vote on the charter revision proposals. The legislature rejected the aldermen's appeal for a popular vote and approved the provisions. Still, it took a few years before their impact was realized. Despite the charter changes and the imposition of citywide voting, in 1899, the slate of aldermanic candidates supported by the ward leaders won every seat.[44] But that would be their last electoral sweep. In the hotly contested 1901 elections, the business elite could claim a small victory when one of their candidates was elected.

An amendment to the city charter after the 1901 election produced another and more unusual adjustment to the Austin City Council. As well as electing seven aldermen at-large, voters within each of the seven wards would also elect an alderman from that ward. Thus, the council doubled in size and included aldermen elected citywide and from wards. Three series of council elections—1903, 1905, and 1907—were conducted in this way. Meanwhile, a group of prominent merchants formed the Business League with the express purpose of recruiting and promoting candidates for the council.[45] Over time, the influence of the Business League grew, and Austin's aldermen increasingly included attorneys, bankers, and owners of large retail establishments within their ranks.

The frequent structural changes to Austin's council and the shift in the composition of the council set the stage for a more audacious charter reform proposal in 1909: commission government. Since being adopted in Galveston in 1901, commission government had spread rapidly throughout Texas in the first decade of the twentieth century, with Houston adopting the plan in 1905 and Dallas, Fort Worth, and El Paso following suit in 1907.[46] The structure merges the legislative and executive functions of city government into a city commission: "As a group, the commissioners constitute the legislative body of the city responsible for taxation, appropriations, ordinances, and other general functions. Individually, each commissioner is in charge of a specific aspect of municipal affairs, e.g., public works, finance, or public safety."[47] The position of mayor varied: in some cities, one commissioner would take on the mayoral role, in others the mayor was elected as mayor-commissioner. Regardless, there was no true chief executive and the mayoral job itself was primarily ceremonial. The commission system was part of a larger Progressive Era effort at reforming government, especially local government, intended to make it function more effectively and efficiently. All told, approximately five hundred U.S. cities adopted the commission form before enthusiasm for it began to diminish after World War I.

In Austin in 1908, after a spirited campaign in which the Business League played a major role, the city's electorate was given the opportunity to vote on replacing the mayor/aldermanic form with a commission government structure. Proponents of the change argued that a commission form of government would lead to improved public services at lower or equal tax prices. In addition, a commission structure would facilitate greater growth and prosperity in Austin while retention of a ward system was said to unnecessarily politicize city government and dampen growth. Their opponents, many aldermen among them, contended that such a change would be costly and that insufficient evidence existed to support the proponents' claims of the benefits of the commission form.[48] The charter revision, which also included a provision for initiative and referendum, was approved by a 2–1 margin. This result can be attributed in part to high levels of spending by business leaders in support of the measure and low voter turnout overall.

Austin's commission government possessed many of the features of other commission governments including nonpartisan, at-large elections of the commissioners. Each commissioner was in charge of a specific department, in Austin the departments were Public Affairs; Receipts, Disbursements, and Accounts; Parks and Public Property; Streets and Public Improvements; and Police and Public Safety.[49] The commissioner in charge of the Public Affairs Department served as mayor. The term of office was two years with commissioners being paid $2,000 annually and the mayor $2,500.[50] And, although the elections were formally nonpartisan, slating groups often mobilized to recruit and promote certain candidates. For example, in the first commission election in 1909, the "Citizens' Committee for the People's Charter" assembled a ticket for the commission consisting of the "upper crust of the business community," notably individuals involved in the growth industry.[51]

One predictable outcome of the commission structure was that, upon taking office, commissioners became advocates for their own departments. This generated rivalries within the commission that could be difficult to resolve especially given the lack of a chief executive. In Austin, this problem was ameliorated somewhat by the election of A. P. Wooldridge as mayor in 1909, a banker willing and able to play a leadership role, but when he left office in 1919 the stress cracks in the commission structure deepened. The ambitious efforts to develop the city, which included extensive infrastructure investment, began to stall. The business community increasingly became dissatisfied with the commission's ability to govern effectively. By 1920, the Austin Chamber of Commerce—the successor to the Business League—was withdrawing its support for the commission structure and searching for an alternative reform structure. A new organization, the City Manager Club, was established to take the lead in an effort to replace the commission form with a new structure: the council-manager form.

The City Manager Club worked assiduously to promote the reform, citing the advantages of a city government run more like a business. It was not an easy sell. Longtime political leader, Andrew Zilker, once an opponent of the change to a commission form had become one of its ardent supporters. He and others established the Commission Government League to support the retention of the commission form. But commission adherents were swimming against a rising tide as cities around the state reconsidered their embrace of commissions. Even though a council-manager structure retained many of the features of a commission government, such as at-large, nonpartisan elections, it represented a very different way of governing Austin. As with any institutional change, there would be winners and losers. The eventual approval of a council-manager form in Austin came after a sustained battle between reformers and those favoring the status quo.

The Council-Manager Form of Government

In 1924, Austin voters narrowly approved a charter revision that would put an end to the commission form of government by adopting a council-manager structure.[52] In five former wards, support for continuation of the commission form prevailed, but the size of the pro–council-manager vote in the two so-called silk stocking former wards was sufficient to secure victory.[53] No longer would the legislative and executive functions of city government be merged; under a council-manager form, the council hires a manager to administer the operation of city government. The council adopts policies; the manager and the administrative staff implement those policies. In theory, politics and administration are separate. A city manager's role is extensive and includes appointing and removing department heads, overseeing service delivery, researching issues and advising the council about them, and preparing budget proposals for the council to consider. In practice, the line between politics and administration can become blurred and separation chimerical.

Despite voter approval of the council-manager structure, opposition from the sitting commission government led to a two-year delay in its implementation. Only after protracted litigation did commissioners, in 1926, consent to scheduling an election for a new council. At that election, the candidates endorsed by the City Manager Club were victorious. Once they took office, the new council expanded municipal functions and embarked upon an ambitious program of civic development.[54] The underlying motivation was growth and prosperity. The City Manager Club renamed itself with a more unifying, action-oriented moniker, "Onward Austin," and unleashed an aggressive campaign to generate support for a major bond issue. The measure passed with a two-thirds majority; business management prevailed at city hall.

Even when Zilker's forces were able to win control of a majority of seats on the council in 1933, and a Zilker protégé, Tom Miller, was elected mayor, the twin themes of growth and prosperity remained firmly entrenched.[55] In her historical study of southwestern cities, political scientist Amy Bridges refers to Zilker and Miller as "sunbelt centralizers," leaders who "claimed to be opponents of municipal reform, appealed to working people and citizens of color, built political organizations, and were skillful in the pursuit of ambitious growth strategies for their cities."[56] Regardless of who actually occupied council seats, business interests, particularly those connected to development, continued to be influential in the city. On occasion, voices of opposition emerged such as liberal Democrats Emma Long and Ben White who served on the council in the 1950s and 1960s, but the governing coalition in mid-twentieth century Austin was reliably conservative in its outlook.[57]

Three Other Charter Changes

Austin city government continues to operate with a council-manager form of government to this day. Elections for mayor and council are nonpartisan, and, until 2014, council elections were at-large. Three charter changes enacted between 1953 and 1969 have had a direct and significant impact on the city council: creating a place system for at-large elections, expanding the size of the council, and providing for the direct election of the mayor. It was in January 1953 that voters approved a revision to the charter establishing a place system for at-large city council races. In a place system, candidates compete citywide for specific council seats designated by a number. Therefore, each candidate runs against only the candidates seeking that place. These city council places were not linked to a specific geographic area and voters living anywhere in the city could vote for a candidate in each of the five places. To win, a candidate had to receive a majority of the votes cast for that place, and, if this did not happen, then a runoff election was held between the top-two vote getters for the seat. The more candidates competing, the greater the likelihood of a runoff.[58] The use of runoffs has myriad consequences, including ensuring that the winner receives a majority of the votes cast, increasing the cost of administering elections, and attracting an often much lower rate of voter participation.

Imposing a place mechanism on an at-large election helps manage the competition; rather than candidates running against everyone else in a complete winner take all format, candidates compete against specific opponents. It generates intense strategizing among potential candidates as they decide which one of the places they wish to seek. It also advantages citywide organizations promoting a slate of candidates in that they can target specific seats for their candidates thereby keeping them from running against each other.[59] According to sociologist Anthony Orum, at least one of the rationales for the promotion of the place proposition in Austin was to prevent the reelection of Councilwoman Emma Long.[60] The first woman to run for and be elected to the Austin City Council in 1948, Long, with her vocal concern for the needs of Austin's poor residents and her active support of labor unions, had proven to be a thorn in the side of land developers and major business interests. They were unabashed in their desire to get her off of the council, and more money was spent in an effort to defeat her than had ever been spent in prior council races.[61] But it was to no avail as Councilwoman Long survived the challenge in 1953, and, popular with the public, she won several subsequent elections for the Place 1 seat. Some historians have suggested that another motivating factor in the adoption of a place system was to make it more difficult for blacks to be elected to the council.[62]

In 1967, three-quarters of Austin voters approved a revision to the charter to increase the size of the city council from five to seven members to take effect in the 1969 council elections. The city's population was increasing rapidly, and, to many Austinites, enlarging the council seemed a logical consequence. However, that was not the only rationale for the proposed change. Some supporters of the expansion believed that a larger governing body would hinder the ability of liberals to gain control of the council.[63] The 1969 election included a charter revision proposition that would provide for direct election of the mayor, beginning in 1971. This change too was attributed to the city's growth. In smaller cities, it was common for the council to select the mayor from among its ranks, but, in big cities, voters elected their mayors. The measure was approved with 85 percent of the vote. Even when directly elected, as a council-manager city, Austin's mayor would remain a member of council.[64]

The Council Shifts Left . . . Most of the Time

In 1973, Austin voters considered—and rejected—a plan to add single member districts to its at-large city council. It was the first of many attempts to alter the representational system used to elect the Austin City Council, a topic that is pursued in detail in Chapter 2. For the council, the late 1960s and the 1970s saw many changes. In 1967, by a 3–2 vote, the council had passed a fair housing ordinance aimed at ending racial discrimination in the sale or rental of property. When given a chance to vote on the issue, the Austin electorate rejected the ordinance and when the next election rolled around, they defeated the three council members who had supported it. But it was a time of unrest in much of urban America, and, in Austin, the lowering of the voting age to eighteen in 1971 propelled many college and university students into local politics. In the early 1970s, many of the newly enfranchised students joined forces with liberal groups and with black and Hispanic residents of East Austin and went about registering large numbers of new voters. Candidates endorsed by the Greater Austin Association, a coalition of progrowth businessmen, started encountering credible challenges from candidates backed by the liberal Coalition for a Progressive Austin.[65] The dominance of progrowth interests in city politics began to weaken. In 1975, liberals won five seats on the seven-member Austin City Council, including the election of avowed liberal and recent graduate of the law school at the University of Texas, Jeff Friedman, to the mayor's office. This change in the composition of Austin's council was effected by the solid turnout among groups that had not been regular participants in Austin city elections in the past.[66] Their mobilization made the difference. The change in the ideological makeup of the council did not lead to wholesale reversals of city policy, but it did produce some notable changes, such as the adoption of the Austin Tomorrow Plan in 1979, intended to channel growth into specific corridors and away from sensitive environmental areas.

From the 1970s to 2012, there were no significant structural adjustments to the city council, except for the imposition of term limits on council members. As for ideology, the governing body has tended toward a moderate to liberal stance. Occasional shifts to the right occurred, with the development-friendly councils of 1983 and 1991 as cases in point, but, in both instances, they were followed by the election of more left-leaning councils.[67]

The Austin Tomorrow Plan with its growth-management emphasis proved easier to draft than to implement. The issue of growth has continued to spark debate, basically how much growth and where new development should occur. Amid significant opposition to "Houstonizing Austin," city officials welcomed the tech boom of the 1980s and the money that poured into the community. But the tech boom put tremendous growth pressure on the city's infrastructure and environment. As discussed in the Introduction, environmental causes such as the 1992 Save Our Springs initiative crystallized the backlash against growth, and, even though the legislature eviscerated the Save Our Springs ordinance, real estate interests and business groups in Austin tacitly acknowledged the need to work with local environmentalists.[68] This ushered in an era of what might be called "reluctant conciliation" among the opposing forces.

The results of the 1997 election produced what became known as the Green Council, and from that came the SGI. Since then, the city has pursued a pro-

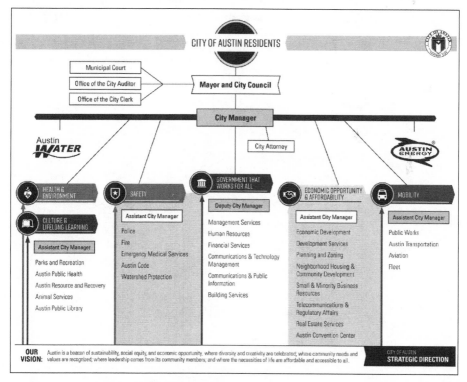

Figure 1.2. Organization chart, city of Austin.

(Source: City of Austin, accessed May 1, 2019, available at http://www.austintexas.gov/sites/default/files/files/City_Manager/COAOrgChart02_04_2019.pdf.)

gram of neighborhood planning and reform of the development code to facilitate infill, densification, and transit-oriented mixed-use projects, with the intent of reducing growth pressures in environmentally sensitive areas.[69] One consequence of these efforts was the rapid, and seemingly endless, redevelopment of the downtown area. Another was the accelerated gentrification of East Austin, which spurred the displacement of people of color, a trend that continues to this day.[70] In the meantime, Austin's council-manager system matured, and city government expanded its range of functions and increased its level of sophistication. By 2018, the city was operating with a budget of approximately $3.9 billion dollars, fourteen thousand employees, and nearly one hundred citizen boards, commissions, and task forces.[71] Austin's formal organization chart is shown in Figure 1.2. Of note is the restructuring of city departments and offices into divisions that align with the city's overarching priorities. The city is led by an eleven-member city council that, save for the mayor, represents geographic districts rather than the city as a whole. The complicated story of Austin's shift from a seven-member council elected at-large to an eleven-member district-based council is the subject of Chapter 2.

AUSTIN AND THE LONG ROAD TO CITY
COUNCIL DISTRICTS

O n November 6, 2012, the city of Austin, Texas, held an election. Voters not only had a presidential election, congressional races, and various state and county elective offices on their ballots; they had eighteen "yes" or "no" city propositions to consider. Seven of the propositions
dealt with the issuance of bonds for various facility improvements, the remainder proposed changes to the city charter including two intended to fun-
damentally alter representation in the city. Proposition 3 asked whether the
city charter should be amended to provide for the election of council members from ten geographic single-member districts, with the mayor to be elected citywide. Proposition 4 was similar but proposed that eight council members be elected from geographic single-member districts with the mayor and
two additional council members elected at large. After forty years and six
failed attempts at achieving geographic representation, the voters of Austin
approved not only one but both district propositions. For more than a century, Austin had elected its city council members at large; going forward they
would be elected from districts. A cadre of long-suffering supporters of council districts rejoiced when the results of the election were announced.

This chapter explores why Austin adopted districts after repeated attempts
to do so were rejected by voters. It retraces the long history of failed efforts
and focuses on the concerted endeavors of prodistrict groups to make adoption of a district system a reality. The chapter also describes the process by
which district mapmakers and line drawers went about their work to create
viable "minority opportunity districts" to increase the likelihood that Afri-

can American and Hispanic voters would be able to elect their preferred candidates to the city council.

A Forty-Year Flirtation with Districts

Austin's city charter contains a provision for a citizen initiative, a petitioning process that allows local residents to place an issue on the ballot for a public vote. It requires that a prescribed number of valid signatures be gathered on petitions and submitted to the city clerk for review. If sufficient valid signatures have been collected and no legal issues exist, the question will appear on the ballot for a "yes" or "no" vote by Austin's electorate. In 1971, a petition to put the issue of district representation on the ballot failed to gain the requisite number of signatures, but it marked the beginning of a four-decade effort to change the way Austin elects its city council members. Another noteworthy event in 1971 was the election of Berl Handcox to the Austin City Council—the first African American since Reconstruction to win a seat on the governing body.

The Austin City Council has the authority to create a nonpartisan Charter Revision Committee (CRC) to study and propose amendments to the city's charter. If the council agrees with the CRC's recommendations, these amendments will appear on the ballot for consideration by the electorate. Prior to impaneling a CRC in 1971, it had been nearly two decades since a comprehensive, in-depth study of each section and article of the charter had been undertaken. After holding a series of meetings to get input from numerous community groups and local citizens, the CRC recommended that fourteen propositions be placed on the April 1973 ballot. Several of the propositions dealt directly with the city council, including lowering the age requirements for serving on the council, paying council members a salary of $100 per week, and opening council meetings to the public. But the major item on the 1973 ballot, Proposition 1, would have enlarged the council to eleven seats and required the election of four council members and the mayor citywide and the election of six council members from geographically determined districts. Proposition 1 ran afoul of the powerful Austin Chamber of Commerce and the city's influential newspaper, the *Austin American-Statesman*, both of which were satisfied with the city's existing at-large electoral system. The proposal to create a hybrid electoral system with both district and at-large seats failed, with only 37 percent of voters voting "yes." In fact, only one of the propositions relating to the structure and operation of the city council passed: the provision for open meetings, which 88 percent of the voters favored.[1]

The defeat in 1973 was just the first of many rejections of measures to establish a district-based system for electing some or all city council members. The issue bubbled up again in 1975, when a Citizens' Charter Study Committee (in effect, a CRC by another name) created by the council recommended that the charter be amended to provide for district representation. Within the committee, the debate about districts was not about establishing them; it was about the number that should be created. A majority of the committee supported a 10–1 plan wherein ten council members would be elected by districts and the mayor elected at large. Others on the committee preferred a smaller council and an 8–1 arrangement. Despite the support for districts, a procedural complication related to state law kept the question from being placed before the voters at that time.[2] Notably, in the 1975 election, John Treviño became the first Hispanic elected to the Austin City Council.

Meanwhile, in Other Large Cities in Texas

While all of this was happening in Austin, other cities in Texas were experiencing pressure from groups representing racial and ethnic minorities to switch to district elections. Both San Antonio and Fort Worth adopted district electoral systems in 1977; Houston, Dallas, and El Paso switched to districts two years later.[3] Most of the actions to adopt a district system in these cities were taken in reaction to or in anticipation of legal challenges brought under the federal Voting Rights Act. Table 2.1 compares several features of the city councils of these cities. Five of them operate with a council-manager form of government; Houston is the only large Texas municipality with a mayor-council form. Council size varies as do council members' salaries. As shown in the last column of the table, big Texas cities have enlarged their councils, primarily to accommodate rapid population growth.

The San Antonio case is instructive. The city annexed eighty square miles of land between 1970 and 1974, mostly on the north side of the city and much of it occupied by Anglos. Mexican Americans comprised just over half of the city's population at that time, and these annexations diluted their voting strength.[4] Citing provisions of the Voting Rights Act and detailing the negative effects of the annexations, groups such as the Mexican American Legal Defense and Educational Fund (MALDEF) made their case to the U.S. Department of Justice. Receptive to their arguments, the Department of Justice intervened, telling the city of San Antonio that the annexations could not go forward unless the city came up with an offsetting remedy: an electoral system that included single-member districts.[5] The city council put a 10–1

TABLE 2.1. LARGE TEXAS CITIES: GOVERNMENT FORM AND CITY COUNCIL CHARACTERISTICS

City	Current form of government (year adopted)	Year district elections adopted	Number of city council seats	Council member annual salary	Most recent adjustment to council configuration (year)
Austin	Council-Manager (1924)	2012	11 (10 + mayor)	$76,086	Changed from at large to districts, added four seats (2012)
Dallas	Council-Manager (1930)	1979	15 (14 + mayor)	$60,000	Added four seats, replaced three remaining at-large seats with district seats (1990)
El Paso	Council-Manager (2004)	1979	9 (8 + mayor)	$29,000	Added two seats (1993)
Fort Worth	Council-Manager (1924)	1977	9 (8 + mayor	$25,002	Will add two seats after 2020 census (2016)
Houston	Mayor-Council (1946)	1979	16*	$62,983	Added two seats (2012)
San Antonio	Council-Manager (1951)	1977	11 (10 + mayor)	$45,722	Changed from at large to districts (1977)

Sources: Data from individual city websites, accessed April 25, 2018, available at http://www.austintexas.gov/; https://dallascityhall.com/; https://www.elpasotexas.gov/; https://fortworthtexas.gov/; http://www.houstontx.gov/; https://www.sanantonio.gov/.

* Houston's city council consists of eleven council members elected from districts and five council members elected at large. The mayor is not a member of the council but he or she presides over council meetings and has a vote in council deliberations.

district plan on the 1977 ballot, and, by a narrow margin, it was approved by voters.[6] Later that year, council elections under the new 10–1 system produced a diverse council of five Mexican Americans, five Anglos, and one African American.

Austin and the "Gentlemen's Agreement"

As the San Antonio case was unfolding, Austin was dealing with its own issues related to the Voting Rights Act. One issue was the so-called gentlemen's agreement, an arrangement worked out by Austin's power brokers that, in practice, reserved one council seat on the seven-member at-large council for an African American and one seat for a Hispanic.[7] This agreement does not appear to have been written down anywhere but numerous observers of

Austin's city politics over the years attest to the existence of such an agreement.[8] And, with few exceptions, that is what ensued in subsequent elections: one black candidate and one Hispanic candidate would be recruited by the business community, supported, and elected. As described in Chapter 1, Austin's at-large system in which candidates competed citywide for specific places on the council facilitated this strategy.

Another issue was a federal lawsuit filed in 1976 by the National Association for the Advancement of Colored People (NAACP) and MALDEF claiming that Austin's at-large electoral system discriminated against minorities. A U.S. district judge heard testimony but was unpersuaded by the arguments of the plaintiffs. When these groups claimed that the at-large system hindered the election of blacks or Hispanics to the council, defenders of the at-large system would point to the presence of one black and one Hispanic on the council. This approach proved to be a successful defense. In the 1970s, African Americans comprised approximately 12 percent of Austin's population, Hispanics approximately 14.5 percent. Those defending the city contended that because the two minorities occupied 28 percent of the council seats—roughly proportional to their population share—there was no violation of the Voting Rights Act.[9]

A closer examination of the operation of the gentlemen's agreement shows that, although two of the seven seats were won by minorities, those candidates were not necessarily the minority groups' choice. The description by a longtime Austin lobbyist lays out the situation: "White Austin politicos hand-picked minorities to run on a slate of candidates, deliberately shutting out from fundraising and endorsements other minority candidates who had deeper roots in the African American and Hispanic communities."[10] In other words, descriptive representation may have been achieved, but it was not as if minority communities were electing candidates of their choosing.

Austin Votes on Districts Again . . . and Again

In April 1978, another district plan was put before the voters, and it was rejected by a wider margin (28 percent in favor and 72 percent opposed) than in the 1973 vote. The plan called for eight council members to be elected by districts, with a citywide vote for mayor. There were no candidate elections on the 1978 ballot, only five charter revision propositions, and turnout was low: 20 percent of registered voters participated in the election.[11] Moreover, an active campaign against the district plan by some members of the city council helped seal its fate.[12]

In 1983, the city council created another CRC to revisit the question of district elections, among a series of other council-related issues. Like earlier and later CRCs, the membership of the 1983 CRC included prominent Austinites, individuals active in civic affairs and local politics. As the CRC undertook its work, another lawsuit was filed in U.S. district court challenging Austin's at-large electoral system. The city council agreed to settle the suit and establish districts. However, the U.S. district judge assigned to the case refused to concur and instead ruled that the at-large system met the constitutional test; the appellate court agreed.[13] With a majority of the council believing that the matter deserved a public vote, an 8–1 district proposal was put on the January 1985 ballot, only for it to be defeated by voters: 43 percent voting "yes," and 57 percent voting "no." One other council-related change was barely approved by voters with an affirmative vote of 51 percent: a charter revision proposition calling for staggered three-year terms for the governing body.

In May 1988, the 8–1 plan returned to the ballot. This time a different set of provisions was included within the 8–1 proposition. The comprehensive ballot measure also called for the creation of a citizens' commission that would make recommendations to the council about how the city would be divided into districts. In addition, the terms for council members would be reduced to two years.[14] The provisions may have been different, but the electoral result was not: voters rejected the 8–1 proposition by the same margin as in 1985: 43 percent in favor and 57 percent opposed.

Clearly, a pattern was developing, one that, regardless of the specifics of the district plan, showed voters were not receptive. The argument voiced by opponents, much of it coming from the Chamber of Commerce and related groups, was that district-based council members were more likely to have parochial interests while those elected at-large would bring more of a city-wide perspective to policy making and problem solving.[15] Some of the lack of enthusiasm appears to have been a perception on the part of many Austinites that "if it ain't broke, don't fix it." But district advocates could take heart in the fact that, even though the measures were defeated each time, the level of opposition was lower in the 1980s-era elections than it had been in the two elections occurring in the 1970s. Some of the failure could be attributed to the timing of the elections. Of the four attempts to get districts approved in the 1970s and 1980s, two of them were in elections in which there were no candidates on the ballot, just propositions. Like other city of Austin elections, they took place outside the regular election cycle for federal and state offices. Although one could argue that the absence of candidates might eliminate distractions, the more likely consequence was a low level of interest among the citizenry. The average turnout for the two proposition-only elections was 24.5 percent of the registered voters.

The 1990s brought the appointment of two more CRCs (in 1990 and 1993) and one more vote on a district plan (in May 1994). And one more defeat for geographic representation in Austin. The 1994 ballot was long with three contested council races and the mayor's seat and twenty-two propositions presented to voters. Austin voters were in an agreeable mood, the majority voting "yes" on nineteen of the propositions. However, one of the three defeated propositions was an 8–1 district plan. This time, the proposition also stated that the districts would be determined by a five-member independent commission and be subject to council approval. In the 1994 election, 26 percent of registered voters participated and the margin of defeat had narrowed significantly (48 percent in favor and 52 percent opposed), giving proponents some hope that victory was close at hand. Despite the rejection of districts, voters reined in the at-large council in two significant ways. First, they approved a measure to limit the terms of the mayor and council members to two consecutive terms unless a subsequent candidacy was supported by a petition of 5 percent of qualified voters.[16] Second, they reduced the amount of time for council review of citizen initiative and referendum petitions and limited the council's option to put alternatives to the petitioned proposal on the ballot.[17]

Although the city council established a CRC in 1997 and discussion ensued about scheduling another vote on a district plan, little movement occurred until 2000 when the CRC recommended that the council place a 10–1 plan on the ballot that year. The *Austin American-Statesman*, which had supported some earlier efforts at creating districts and opposed others, editorialized in favor, calling it "a way to better representation."[18] Several other recommendations were included in the CRC report, such as one calling for an independent redistricting committee to be appointed by the city council to design the new districts and handle subsequent redistricting.[19] There was much speculation about what districts might look like, even if only an approximation, and concerns were voiced that, in a fast-growing city like Austin, population information from the 1990 census had become outdated. Consequently, the council decided to wait until after the 2000 U.S. census was conducted to schedule the next vote on districts.

Another CRC was created in 2001 to review the recommendations of the previous CRC and develop ballot propositions. Instead of a 10–1 plan, the council put a mixed 8–2–1 plan on the May 2002 ballot: eight council members would be elected from geographic districts and two council members and the mayor would be elected citywide. The plan attracted support from some members of the business community, but the *Austin American-Statesman* argued against the plan, calling it "flawed" and a "mish-mash."[20]

The election featured three contested council races and eight propositions, but, despite that, voter turnout was low to the point of dismal: only 9 percent of registered voters participated. Voters rejected the district plan with 42 percent in favor and 58 percent opposed. Provisions to repeal council term limits and provide for a public financing system for council campaigns also went down to defeat. Stung by the defeat, district supporters stepped back, and the momentum for districts stalled. Six years later, in 2008, discussion of districts reemerged yet again. The council was evenly split on whether to place the district question on the ballot again; the mayor was the swing vote on the decision, and he voted "no." Figure 2.1 tracks Austin's consideration of major changes to the city council.

Why the District Proposals Failed

Each of the six attempts had its own set of special circumstances contributing to its failure at the hands of Austin's voters. For example, the earliest effort, in 1973, would have created an eleven-member governing body just four years after the council had expanded from five to seven members. Eleven was perceived as simply too large for Austin, at that time a city of 290,000 residents. Plus, local elites argued against a change to districts, citing the potential for reversion to ward politics. Prior to the pivotal vote in 2012, a review of past failures identified some other idiosyncratic factors.[21] In the lead-up to voting on the 1978 proposition, several members of the city council voiced their opposition to district representation arguing that it would polarize the city. In 1985, the question of districts ran into the buzz saw that was the Chamber of Commerce's well-funded opposition campaign. The 1988 district question was overshadowed by a contentious mayoral race and soft-pedaled by the council. In 1994, the effort that came the closest to victory, supporters planned to explicitly link a district referendum to council term limits, thereby increasing the odds for passage, but the council demurred on the term limits issue. As a stand-alone proposition, the district question could not find its footing. Finally, in 2002, with the Chamber of Commerce and the Real Estate Council of Austin on board with the district concept, it was the proposition for public financing that attracted the greatest attention among Austinites. At public meetings about the district idea, "the silence is deafening," according to one news account. "Neighborhoods that would benefit are ambivalent or apathetic. . . . People are barely talking about it."[22]

There were also debates among advocates about strategy. Should the issue be placed on a regular election ballot or, instead, be considered in a special

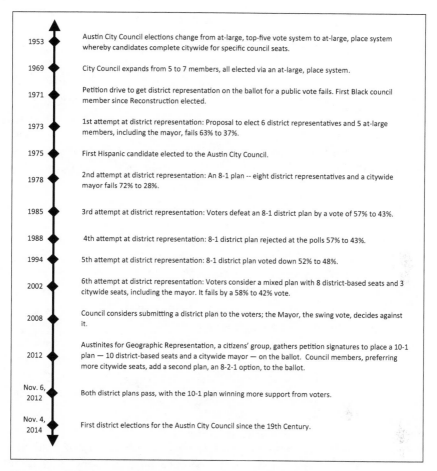

Figure 2.1. Key events in Austin's time line to council districts.

(Source: Created by the author using data from Office of the City Clerk, City of Austin, Election History, accessed March 24–29, 2018, available at http://www.ci.austin.tx.us /election/search.cfm.)

election? Should proponents of district representation sketch out hypothetical districts to show where the lines might be drawn or did that risk getting the cart before the horse? Throughout these failed attempts at adopting a district system, precincts in East Austin voted in favor of districts, but their electoral impact was outstripped by heavy turnout in Austin's politically active central city precincts and in West Austin, where the sentiment for districts was less favorable.

That brings us to 2012. This time the outcome would be different.

2012: Flirtation Gives Way to Commitment

For the most part, the gentlemen's agreement had performed as expected during the forty-year period between the city's first vote on geographic districts in 1973 and the final one in 2012: an African American held one of the council seats, and a Hispanic held another. David Van Os, an attorney for the NAACP's challenges to Austin's at-large system, has said that the agreement was not intended to cede "representation to the communities of color, it was for the purpose of maintaining the at-large system . . . business interests wanted (this) because they believed maintaining the requirement for candidates to campaign citywide would maintain the need for business money to run campaigns and thus keep promoting the elections of candidates friendly to the business interests."[23]

Austin's at-large system, with its two "reserved" places, continued long after other Texas cities' had switched to district elections. But, by the early 2000s, the gentlemen's agreement had begun to slip as more challengers sought those designated seats. Also, the Hispanic community was growing rapidly—by 2010, Hispanics comprised 35 percent of the population—and the allotment of one council seat no longer seemed sufficient.[24]

There was another, perhaps not unintended, outcome of the way at-large elections functioned in Austin: most of the council members resided in the same part of the city. The map in Figure 2.2 pinpoints the residential locations of the city council members serving in 2012, superimposed over the districts created in 2013 by the Independent Citizens Redistricting Commission (ICRC). The geographic clustering of council members under the at-large system is apparent: most of the seven council members lived in what became District 9; the remaining council members resided nearby but in what became other districts. The 2012 pattern was not an aberration in that it conformed to other longitudinal analyses of council residential data showing that most council members had lived in Central Austin; seldom did council members live in other parts of the city. The *Austin Bulldog* mapped the residences of those who had served on the city council from 1971 to 2011 and found that 57 percent of those elected lived within three miles of city hall, 26 percent lived from three to five miles from city hall, and 17 percent lived more than five miles from city hall. As the *Austin Bulldog* concluded, "Statistically speaking, this is just another way of saying that political power is highly concentrated within the central city."[25]

Even though legal challenges to Austin's at-large system were not successful, and previous attempts to get voter approval of districts had fallen short, there remained groups of Austinites committed to making geographic representation a reality. In the meantime, a Republican state senator, Jeff

Figure 2.2. Council members' residences, 2012; city council districts, 2014.
(Sources: Map created by Andrew Garrison in Google Maps, using data from the City of Austin, Office of the City Clerk, Ballot Applications; City of Austin, City Council Districts, May 2016, available at http://austintexas.gov/sites/default/files/files/Planning /Demographics/Districts10.pdf.)

Wentworth, introduced a bill in 2009 that would have required that the government of any Texas city with a population of five hundred thousand or more "must consist of a mayor elected at large and at least six members elected from single-member districts."[26] In reality, given that all other Texas cities in this population category had long ago met the requirements, this bill affected Austin, and only Austin. The senator's bill languished in committee but was reintroduced for the 2011 session. There is almost nothing that the Austin community likes less than being told what to do by the state legislature, so the bill generated some urgency along the lines of "let's do this ourselves, rather than having the legislature interfere."

Austinites for Geographic Representation

Some of the folks who were continuing to carry the district banner had been members of a CRC created in 2011 that, after vigorous debate within its ranks, had split 8–7 on the nature of a proposed district plan. The majority recommended a 10–1 plan to the city council, with a minority report favoring a 10–2–1 plan. Seeking to avoid the missteps of the past, many of those who had formed the CRC majority in support of a 10–1 district proposal set about to design and implement an approach that would ultimately be approved by voters. The group that they and others established, Austinites for Geographic Representation (AGR), was the primary force behind the effort at getting a district system approved in 2012.

More than a small streak of populism ran through AGR. The organizers engaged in outreach, uniting diverse groups in the process. Local Democratic and Republican Party organizations, the NAACP, the League of United Latin American Citizens (LULAC), the University of Texas student government, the League of Women Voters, Texans for Accountable Government, the Austin Firefighters Association, and the Austin Neighborhoods Council are but some of the organizations that supported AGR and the 10–1 plan. AGR worked tirelessly over a two-year period building the foundation for another run at the district question. By this point, in the view of some observers, geographic representation had become an emotional issue for numerous Austin progressives.

Five of the six earlier attempts at geographic representation had set the number of district seats at eight. However, AGR's plan set the number at ten, primarily because research indicated that it was the smallest number that would assure the creation of an African American plurality district as well as several Hispanic majority districts.[27] The racial and ethnic demographics of Austin had changed since the 1970s when there was relative parity in the numbers of blacks and Hispanics. According to the 2010 census, African Americans comprised approximately 8.1 percent of the city's population and Hispanics approximately 35.1 percent.

One of AGR's first decisions was to use a petition process and collect signatures to force the city council to put the issue on the ballot. As an AGR insider commented, "The message was easy to sell, proof points were easy to find. Presenting data on the unfairness of the at-large system was enough to sway petition-signers."[28] To qualify for the ballot, AGR had to get approximately twenty thousand valid signatures of registered voters residing in Austin. In July 2012, AGR submitted its petitions to the city clerk with more than enough valid signatures. Meanwhile, in response to the CRC's recommendation, the council had already voted 5–2 to put the issue on the ballot (it would be Proposition 3), but the petition ensured that if the council had a change of heart, the proposition would still appear on the ballot.

Additionally, at the same council meeting, the council had voted 4–3 to put its own district plan on the ballot, to give voters another option. Hearkening back to 2002, it was an 8–2–1 plan with eight council members elected from districts and two council members plus the mayor elected at large. It became Proposition 4. The city's mayor, Lee Leffingwell, and three council members argued that they supported the creation of districts but that their plan retaining two at-large council districts offered a less radical change. In the view of Mayor Leffingwell, "A mixed system of representation, one that incorporates a mix of representatives from districts and citywide representatives, is the best choice for Austin. I believe a mixed system would allow for a fair balance of interests . . . elevating neighborhood-level concerns without abandoning citywide perspectives."[29] Clearly, the city council was anxious to get aboard the suddenly onrushing train that was geographic representation but with the condition that some citywide representation beyond the mayor be retained.

Other arguments in support of the 8–2–1 plan were that the retention of some at-large seats would benefit minority groups that were more dispersed and less geographically concentrated, such as Asians and members of the LGBTQ community.[30] Besides, voters would be able to vote for more council members under a hybrid plan: the council member from their own district, the two at-large council members, and the mayor. Potentially, this could give residents more points of access to the governing body. Others balked at the idea of presenting voters with two options, believing that putting two plans on the ballot would likely doom both of them.[31] The way the ballot was set up, voters could vote on each proposition independently, and, if both received majority support, the plan with more votes would win. If neither had majority support, then it was back to the drawing board for district advocates.

One of the key components of Proposition 3, the 10–1 plan, was the provision for a fourteen-member independent commission of residents that would draw the district lines. This was something that the 2011 CRC had recommended, and it was intended to minimize the likelihood of political gerrymandering of the districts. The approach was borrowed from California's method for its redistricting processes. Prohibited from serving on the independent commission were city council members, anyone who had been a candidate for local or state office in the past five years, paid political workers, city employees, lobbyists, and large campaign donors to city elections. For many people in Austin, the use of an independent commission was a strong selling point of the 10–1 plan.[32] AGR's pitch to voters was to trust this nonpartisan, nonpoliticized commission that would draw lines.[33] In fact, AGR used the phrase "Trust Austin" in much of its promotional literature. This theme is evident in the example of AGR's campaign material featured in Figure 2.3. Proposition 4, the mixed electoral system approach favored by majority of the city council, did not incorporate an independent redistricting commission into its proposition, suggesting to some observers that any line drawing done under Proposition 4 could be subject to council influence.

The formal proposition laid out a detailed process for selecting the independent commission. To serve on the ICRC, a person had to have been a registered voter in Austin for at least five years and have voted in three of the five most recent city general elections. Anyone who met the qualifications—and was not in one of the disqualifying categories—could apply. The applications would be reviewed by an applicant review panel created by the city auditor and composed of three qualified, independent licensed auditors. This panel would identify the sixty most qualified applicants for the ICRC to form the pool from which eight commissioners would be randomly selected.[34] These eight would then select the final six commissioners from the pool, with those selections being reflective of the city's diversity in terms of race, ethnicity, gender, and geography. Those who served on the ICRC would be ineligible for ten years to hold elective office in Austin.

Guidelines for line drawing were spelled out in what was to be an open and transparent process that welcomed full public input. Districts had to be of reasonably equal population, comply with federal and state law, respect the geographic integrity of neighborhoods and communities of interest, and be geographically contiguous and compact, among other requirements. The opposition to gerrymandering is clear in this explicit statement in the guidelines:

> The place of residence of any incumbent or potential political candidate shall not be considered in the creation of a plan or any district. Districts shall not be drawn for the purpose of favoring or discriminating against any incumbent, political candidate, or political group.[35]

AGR's campaign for Proposition 3 was well organized, with hundreds of—perhaps as many as one thousand—volunteers who knocked on doors, made phone calls, put up signs, and spoke at campaign forums. The group

DO YOU LIVE IN THE "RIGHT" PART OF AUSTIN?

Check this map.

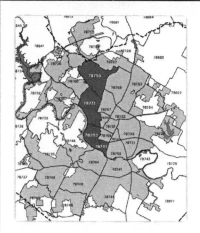

Politically the "right" part of Austin is 4 ZIP codes: 78701, 78703, 78731, 78759.

If you live in those ZIP codes then:
- more than 50% of the City Council Members have lived near you
- 15 of 17 mayors have lived near you

If you don't live in those ZIP codes then:
- you likely don't live near a City Council member
- you very likely don't live near any mayors

Today in Austin politics, where you live decides your influence. For 40 years, more than half of City Council and 15 of 17 mayors lived in the same part of town, home to just 10% of Austinites. Even minority city council members are not elected by minority voters.

THAT'S NOT FAIR!

City Council Members can't fairly represent all of Austin if they all live in only one part of town! Real representation will come when City Council members live where their voters do.

The Proposition 3 plan will give every Austinite a chance to be represented on City Council. Under this plan, every Austinite will live near **THEIR** City Council member.

VOTE **YES** ON PROP 3!

TRUST AUSTIN
VOTE YES ON PROP 3!
Citizens Districting 10-1

BE SURE TO GO DOWN THE BALLOT TO VOTE FOR PROP 3:
- The People's Plan
- 10 neighborhood City Council districts
- An Independent Citizens Commission to draw the district lines!!

WHY VOTE FOR PROP 3?
- Austin is the largest city in the country without geographic representation for its City Council.
- For 40 years, 4 zip codes have elected 50% of council and 15 out of the last 17 mayors. That means that 10% of the population has had 50% of the representation and decides how to spend the other 90%'s tax money. **That's not right!**
- It's time **YOU** help change our unrepresentative and unfair at-large system.

TRUST AUSTIN, VOTE YES ON PROP 3
- 10 geographic districts
- 1 mayor at large
- District lines fairly drawn by an independent commission filled with people like your neighbors – not politicians
- Created by the people for all of Austin: Backed by Democrats and Republicans, Homebuilders and Environmentalists, the Austin Neighborhoods Council, the Charter Revision Commission, the League of Women Voters, Police, Firefighters, and more
- Prop 3 brings truly representative democracy and diversity to Austin City Council

VOTE NO ON PROP 4 — THE POLITICIAN'S PLAN
- Sets up unequal representation
- Will fail the Voting Rights Act
- Council will gerrymander the district lines
- Key supporter is the Real Estate Council of Austin (large real estate investors)

Visit **www.TrustAustin.org** to find out more and how you can get involved.

Paid for by Austinites for Geographic Representation, PAC 6705 Hwy 290 West Suite 502 #173, Austin, TX 78735
www.AustinGeoRep.org   512-692-7644

Figure 2.3. Flyer distributed by Austinites for Geographic Representation.

(Source: Flyer created by Austinites for Geographic Representation using data from the *Austin Bulldog*. Used by permission.)

raised more than \$116,000 to fund its efforts, substantially more than the group backing Proposition 4, Austin Communities for Change (AC4C), as it became known.[36] AC4C counted some of the city's political establishment in its midst, including several individuals who had been part of the 2011 CRC and had been on the losing side of the 8–7 CRC vote on a district plan.[37] Others involved in AC4C included real estate interests, spokespersons for Asian American organizations, a wing of the Greater Austin Chamber of Commerce, the West Austin Democrats organization, and some environmental groups.[38] AC4C's strategy was to make a strong case for a mixed system of representation by emphasizing its balance. Also, some in AC4C's leadership tried to mobilize the environmental community by arguing that Barton Springs, a treasured natural resource for Austinites, would be jeopardized if it were part of a council district won by a conservative, prodevelopment candidate.[39] Barton Springs, it was contended, would be better protected by progressives imbued with a citywide orientation, that is, at-large council members. But AC4C got a late start and did not generate the fervor or widespread support that AGR had developed. For its part, AGR took pains to characterize the two plans as the AGR's "people's plan" versus the AC4C's "politicians' plan." One of AGR's leaders characterized AC4C as "West Austin trying to keep their power in city politics."[40]

On November 6, 2012, the Austin electorate did what it had not done before and approved a district system for the election of council members. Actually, a majority of voters approved both the 10–1 plan and the 8–2–1 plan, but, because the AGR-sponsored plan received more votes than the council-sponsored plan (146,496 vs. 121,741, respectively), it became law. Other relevant propositions winning voter approval included a change in the election dates for the mayor and council from May to November in even-numbered years and four-year staggered terms with a two-term limit. Table 2.2 lists the wording of the propositions, the results of the voting, and the preelection projected financial impacts of the propositions.

Explaining the Success of the 10–1 Proposal

So, why did a district plan pass after forty years and six failed attempts? Some might say that it was just a matter of time, that Austin had been behind the curve on this issue for decades and simply caught up. After all, Austin had changed over forty years, tripling in population and expanding its economy. It had moved into a different tier of cities: it was no longer just a capital city or a university town; it had become one of Richard Florida's creative cities—a place where technology, talent, and tolerance were said to thrive.[41] The city possessed a strong sense of place because of a quality of life that was sought

TABLE 2.2. SELECTED 2012 CHARTER AMENDMENTS: PROJECTED IMPACT AND
ELECTION RESULTS

Proposition	Short description	Total votes for	Total votes in favor (%)	Projected annual impact	Projected 5-year impact (FY 13–FY 17)
1	Move the city's general election date from May to November.	193,901	76.47%	$255,000 Savings per election year	Savings of $765,000
2	Move the city's general election date from May to November, to provide that council members serve four-year staggered terms, to provide that council elections occur in even-numbered years, and to limit the mayor and council members to two terms.	188,883	76.62%	$255,000 Savings per election year	Savings of $1,655,000
3	Provide for the election of council members from ten geographic single-member districts, with the mayor to be elected from the city at large, and to provide for an independent citizens redistricting commission.	146,496	60.16%	$1,396,000 Costs for additional council member and staff salary	Costs of $5,622,000
4	Provide for the election of council members from eight geographic single-member districts, with the mayor and two additional council members to be elected from the city at large.	121,781	51.08%	$1,396,000 Costs for additional council member and staff salary	Costs of $5,622,000

Sources: Ed Van Eenoo, City of Austin, "Memorandum: Assessment of Fiscal Impact for Charter Amendments," August 29, 2012, 1–2; City of Austin, City Clerk, Election Results, accessed February 17, 2018, available at http://www.ci.austin.tx.us/election/byrecord.cfm?eid=196.

after and celebrated. The popular motto "Keep Austin Weird" is a nostalgic plea that captures the extensive changes that have taken place in the city.[42] Austin had grown not simply because of in-migration but also because of the city's annexation of adjacent territory and the population residing there. As shown earlier in Figure 1.1, Austin had expanded its boundaries and brought new residents into its orbit. Now, not only were minority communities supportive of a system that was more representative of them and their interests; many residents in the outlying areas of the city, particularly in the newly annexed areas, were also seeking an electoral system that would produce geographic representation.

Amid the fortuitous timing and changing circumstances, AGR did a number of things right. The leadership of the organization was resolute and smart. They reached out to and were supported by a large number of groups citywide, more than thirty formal organizations. Some of these groups were traditionally opposed to one another, but they saw a district system as beneficial to their disparate interests. Take, for example, LULAC and the Travis County Republican Party. With districts, LULAC could predict with confidence that more Hispanics would be elected to the council, and the Travis County GOP believed that districts increased the odds that conservative candidates could win a seat or two in areas that leaned Republican.[43] AGR was skillful in broadening the definition of "disadvantaged minorities" beyond racial and ethnic groups: any geographically concentrated group that was relatively cohesive could potentially benefit from a district electoral system. This strategic framing of the issue helped build a broad coalition to promote the 10–1 proposal.

Internally, AGR worked to build consensus. The group typically did not take a position or act on an issue until 80–85 percent of member groups were on board.[44] Also, their use of a petition drive to get the district proposition on the ballot put them in front of many potential voters as they knocked on doors and buttonholed shoppers at local malls. This was an effective method for not only bringing attention to the issue; it also signaled that it was a bottom-up rather than a top-down process. The grassroots, neighborhood-based structure of AGR paid dividends.

AGR and its supporters hammered away at the fact that Austin was the largest city in Texas, and, indeed, in the entire country, that did not elect council members from districts.[45] Moreover, the inclusion in Proposition 3 of a provision for the creation of an independent redistricting commission, one that would be devoid of politicians and, it was hoped, less inclined to engage in political gerrymandering, was a compelling factor. AGR also emphasized the relative unfairness of an at-large system, and how in Austin this meant that, for a very long time, city council members had resided in one or two areas of the city. It was not a new revelation that large portions of the city had never elected someone from their area to the council, but it was publicized in myriad ways during the 2012 campaign for districts. Related to this, AGR was adept at utilizing social media and at drawing the attention of traditional media, both broadcast and print. Extensive coverage of AGR's activities appeared in these forums.

Furthermore, AGR faced less entrenched opposition as earlier supporters of the at-large system began to waver. Important among these converts was the business community. Enthusiasm for the at-large system had already weakened in some business circles, notably in the Chamber of Commerce. The reasons for this are not completely clear but growing dissatisfaction with various outcomes of the at-large election process was a factor. Moreover, a belief took hold among some in corporate leadership that Austin's use of an at-large system made the city "look bad," compared to other big cities.[46] Eventually, the idea of a geographically based district system began to be seen as less of a threat to business interests. In fact, to many, a district system was a palatable alternative; that is, they came to realize they could work with a district system, and perhaps even benefit from it. However, a split within the business sector emerged over which district plan was preferable.[47] Emblematic of this division, the Real Estate Council of Austin was more favorably disposed to the 8–2–1 plan and the Austin Home Builders Association supported the 10–1 proposal. The chamber did not take a formal position in favor of one or the other.

Finally, one should not underestimate the importance of the timing of the election. Voting on the district question in November in conjunction with federal and state elections and with a presidential race at the top of the ballot brought more people to the polls. This was not the typical low-turnout city election with only 20 percent or so of the electorate participating and in which the more politically active areas outvoted other parts of Austin. Consider the election six months earlier on May 12, 2012, for the mayor and three city council seats. Turnout of registered voters was a tepid 11 percent. Turnout for the November 6, 2012, election with a presidential election headlining the ballot, along with a U.S. Senate election, congressional races, and state legislative and county races was 60 percent. The seventeen city propositions on the ballot, including several bond measures, were part of a much larger election ballot for Austin voters. The increased level of voter participation that occurs when a presidential election is on the ballot strongly suggests that the composition of Austin's November electorate was different from the May electorate. Most parts of Austin supported the 10–1 plan, but the highest levels of support were found in precincts in South and East Austin and in the outer reaches of North Austin. Voting in favor of the proposition was weakest in West/Central Austin, the areas in which, historically, most at-large council members had resided.[48]

The convergence of these factors contributed to the success of the 10–1 plan in 2012. The euphoria that supporters experienced when geographic representation was approved marked the completion of the first step. Next up was the selection of the ICRC and the drawing of district lines, a process that faced its own set of challenges.

Making Maps and Drawing District Lines

In his study of city redistricting, political scientist Joshua Behr recommends that caution is appropriate when applying assumptions drawn from state-level redistricting to the local level.[49] As he suggests, the political and geographic contexts are different and more intimate in a community. However, at both levels of government, the creation of majority-minority districts is one mechanism that is used regularly to improve the odds that racial and ethnic minorities have a meaningful opportunity to elect their preferred candidates to legislative offices. It does not guarantee their election, of course; other factors such as the amount of competition and the level of voter turnout certainly matter. But rather than stacking the deck against minority candidates through an at-large electoral system, districts can be created that offer minority candidates a realistic chance of winning office.

Behr's research analyzed the impact of districts with different levels of minority voting-age population (50 percent, 55 percent, and 60 percent), which are often referred to as "minority-opportunity districts." He found varying results. In general, his study of 111 cities showed that when a district has a Hispanic voting-age population of 50 percent, Hispanic candidates have a 55 percent probability of being elected. For black candidates competing in a district with a black voting-age population of 50 percent, the probability of being elected is 80 percent.[50] Further, and this is relevant to the Austin case, Behr notes that, at the local level, black candidates often have had electoral success when district percentages are well below 50 percent.

In Austin, the task awaiting the ICRC was to carve up the city into defensible districts with populations of approximately eighty thousand each. As mentioned earlier in the chapter, one of AGR's persistent themes during the campaign for districts was the unfairness of an at-large system, particularly the way it had impeded the ability of racial and ethnic minorities to elect candidates of their choosing. Now, the challenge for the ICRC was to create districts that would make good on the promise of districts. Until a 2013 U.S. Supreme Court decision removed the requirement, communities covered under the federal Voting Rights Act had to have their changes to district lines precleared by the U.S. Department of Justice.[51] In Austin, the initial expectation of the ICRC was that the Justice Department would review their plan under the preclearance provision, but the court ruling made the issue moot. The ICRC's plan would be final.

Perturbed by a slow trickle of applicants for the ICRC, the city redoubled its efforts to generate a deep pool of potential commissioners. Ultimately, more than 500 people applied for the ICRC and, once the applicant review panel eliminated those who were not qualified or had submitted incomplete applications, a pool of 444 viable applicants remained. This was narrowed to the 60 applicants judged most qualified to serve, and, from that group, eight individuals were selected randomly in a process resembling the Powerball lottery. The eight selected then evaluated the applications of the remaining 52 people in the pool to choose the final six members. A key consideration in making the final selections was to diversify the ICRC in terms of member demographics and residential location.

The fourteen-member ICRC by its own account "spent countless hours ensuring that our process was fair and impartial."[52] The hours may not have been counted, but ICRC held forty open meetings and fourteen public hearings in different parts of the city and solicited written and verbal testimony. "The input received by the Commission included 532 in-person testimonials given in 3-minute sessions from 418 Austin residents, 7 invited presentations involving 22 individuals, and 566 emails or letters from Austinites."[53] In other words, the level of public engagement in the process was relatively high. Plenty of local folks had ideas about where the lines should be drawn and which neighborhoods should be included in which districts. Additionally, the availability of mapping software made amateur cartographers out of many interested citizens.

The process did not unfold smoothly, which, given what was at stake, is not surprising. Some ardent 10–1 supporters clashed with the city council and with the ICRC over the pace of their work and details of their process.[54] The ICRC hired staff and also utilized the skills of the city demographer in undertaking its work. It took six months and the map drafted by the ICRC underwent numerous iterations, with the final version containing one African American opportunity district (District 1: 28.2 percent African American) and three Hispanic opportunity districts (District 2: 69.0 percent Hispanic; District 3: 60.8 percent Hispanic; District 4: 65.2 percent Hispanic).[55] The remaining six districts were majority Anglo, that is, non-Hispanic white. There was even one "student opportunity district" in which college and university students made up approximately 45 percent of the district (District 9). The districts drawn by the ICRC met the guidelines specified in the proposition, and they varied with regard to numerous demographic and socioeconomic characteristics. Table 2.3 profiles the ten districts with regard to eight of these characteristics. Besides the racial and ethnic variations, also notable are the ranges in median family income (from $36,185 in District 3 to $131,100 in District 10), the poverty rate (from 6.3 percent in District 6 to 36.4 percent in District 3), the level of education (from 17.8 percent with a bachelor's degree in District 2 to 73.7 percent in District 10), and the unemployment rate (from 4.6 percent in District 8 to 10 percent in District 3).

TABLE 2.3. DEMOGRAPHIC AND SOCIOECONOMIC PROFILES OF AUSTIN'S CITY COUNCIL DISTRICTS WHEN CREATED, 2013									
District (geographic location)	Median family income ($)	Poverty rate (%)	Bachelor's degree, age 25 and above (%)	Unemployment rate (%)	Labor force participation (%)	Anglo (non-Hispanic white) (%)	African American (%)	Hispanics (%)	Asian (%)
District 1 (East Austin)	42,150	27.6	23.8	8.9	69.8	23.3	28.2	43.2	3.3
District 2 (Southeast Austin)	42,650	24.8	17.8	9.5	72.5	20.3	8.0	69.0	1.2
District 3 (East Austin)	36,185	36.4	26.8	10.0	74.2	26.6	8.0	60.8	2.8
District 4 (Central/East Austin)	39,200	31.2	22.0	9.9	75.5	20.8	9.5	65.2	3.0
District 5 (South Austin)	77,250	12.0	43.3	6.7	77.9	59.5	4.2	31.0	2.9
District 6 (Northwest Austin)	85,950	6.3	52.3	6.0	77.4	64.4	4.4	15.1	13.3
District 7 (North Austin)	74,250	12.9	47.8	6.7	78.1	57.6	7.8	22.4	9.6
District 8 (Southwest Austin)	116,150	4.9	64.8	4.6	72.0	69.7	2.2	17.7	8.0
District 9 (Central Austin)	81,535	32.5	68.4	8.7	64.1	66.8	3.5	17.2	9.9
District 10 (West Austin)	131,100	7.8	73.7	5.2	71.0	78.3	1.7	9.3	8.6

Source: City of Austin, District Demographics and Maps, accessed March 22, 2018, available at http://www.austintexas.gov//page/district-demographics.

With the map formally transmitted to the city council, it was on to the 2014 city council elections, an opportunity to gauge the impact of the significant change in how Austin voters select their governing body. Would district supporters' expectations be realized in the election outcomes? And, once the brand-new council took office, would its operation and actions take the city in a different direction? These questions about outcomes are pursued in Chapter 3.

THE IMPACT OF COUNCIL ELECTORAL CHANGE

Once the outlines of the initial district maps were made public, potential candidates began to contemplate the 2014 city council elections, which, for the first time since the nineteenth century, candidates would be running from geographically determined districts. Ten district council seats were available, and candidates would compete without knowing whether, if they won, their initial term of office would be two years or four years. This uncertainty was the result of another proposition approved by voters in 2012 that required staggered council elections with half of the district seats up for election every two years.[1] The length of the first district council members' terms would be decided by lot after the elections. What this meant was that for half of the 2014 winners, the quest for reelection would begin very soon after being sworn in.

In this chapter, the 2014 city election is examined in detail, specifically the level of competition for the seats and the rate of voter turnout. As for the campaigns themselves, many predicted that their costs would be lower than when council campaigns had been citywide in scope. As mentioned in Chapter 2, much was expected of a district-based council: supporters anticipated an array of positive outcomes and opponents forecast many negative consequences. Most prominently, a geographically based district electoral system was expected to diversify council membership and spark a shift in the council agenda. Based on earlier research, another presumption was that council operations would change as a result of the new system and that coalitions within the council could develop. Additionally, with the assumption that differing viewpoints would be present on the council, some anticipated an increase in conflict within the council. This chapter explores the extent to which these outcomes emerged during the first three years of the district council. Of course, drawing hard and fast conclusions is unwarranted from the use of a limited amount of council district data. Media evaluations and public opinion from a citywide poll offer additional perspectives on the performance of Austin's governing body after the switch to districts. The chapter concludes with a discussion of the results of the 2016 and 2018 council elections.

The 2014 City Elections: Candidate Competition and Voter Turnout

As shown earlier in Figure 2.2, most of the 2012 city council members lived in the same part of town, but with two exceptions they were term limited or not seeking reelection in 2014. The two exceptions, Chris Riley and Kathie Tovo, would run against each other and one other candidate for the District 9 seat. As for the other district seats, the candidate floodgates opened. Nine candidates sought the District 1 seat, and District 1 was not an outlier; Districts 4, 7, and 10 each attracted eight candidates; the District 3 seat was the most sought after: twelve candidates filed for it. A total of seventy candidates sought the ten district seats; an average of seven candidates per seat, which far outstrips the level of competition in prior elections. And there were eight candidates seeking the mayor's office, bringing the grand total of candidates on the 2014 city ballot to seventy-eight. One of the goals of instituting district elections was to generate more competition for the seats and give voters more choices, and that goal was certainly accomplished in the first district council election. Of course, unlike an at-large election, an individual voter could vote only in the mayor's race and in the race for the council seat in the district in which the voter lived. Still, there were numerous candidates from which to choose for both of those offices, regardless of the specific council district.

In his study of city elections, political scientist Zoltan Hajnal found that "scheduling local elections to occur on the dates of statewide and national contests has the potential to dramatically alter the existing pattern of local voter turnout."[2] In short, with a presidential election or high-profile statewide races on the ballot, turnout for elections is much higher than it is when the ballot features only local races, especially when those local elections are held off-cycle, typically in the spring. In the hotly contested mayoral and council elections held in April 1971, 56.8 percent of Austin's registered voters participated, but, since then, voter turnout for Austin's city elections, nearly always held in the springtime, had declined significantly.[3] In fact, in no city election since the mid-1990s had voter turnout exceeded the 20 percent mark. Between 2000 and 2012, Austin City Council elections, with or without propositions on the ballot, had generated an average turnout of 10.9 percent for general elections; voter participation in runoff elections was often in the single digits.

Voter turnout in Austin for the November 2014 election was a robust 40.4 percent of registered voters, a far cry from turnout levels in recent city council elections. Statewide elective offices on the ballot, including the governor and a U.S. Senate seat as well as congressional and state legislative races, attracted the highest levels of voter participation. Although some of this surge in turnout is likely attributable to the use of district elections, moving city council elections to the November ballot undoubtedly boosted voter participation.

The increase in voter turnout is noteworthy, but, admittedly, the election was somewhat idiosyncratic. Every council seat including the mayor was on the ballot; and there was some degree of novelty associated with the election given the advent of the district system. Campaigns in several of the districts were hard fought and contentious, and voter interest ran high. That said, district turnout varied, ranging from a high of 44 percent in District 10 to a low of 22.7 percent in District 6.[4]

Runoff elections for city council seats, which were held in December 2014, showed the expected drop-off from the level of participation in the November general election. With the mayor's race and seven council seats in play,[5] the runoff drew 15.6 percent of registered voters to the polls. Despite the relatively low level of participation in the 2014 runoff, the figures exceeded turnout in recent runoff elections under the at-large, place system.

As with many of the outcomes discussed in this chapter, the passage of time will clarify whether the initial effects of the district system have traction for the longer term. The higher levels of candidate competition seen in the 2014 elections gave voters more choice; and, in a related vein, higher rates of turnout facilitate representation.[6] The implications of voter turnout are significant: groups whose members vote regularly are more likely to see their favored candidates win, and, consequently, their preferred policies enacted.[7] After all, as political scientists Chris Tausanovitch and Christopher Warshaw found in their study of public opinion and city policy, "City governments are responsive to the views of their citizens in a wide range of policy areas."[8]

Cost of Campaigning

One of the expected benefits of a district system for candidates is a lowering of the cost of campaigning.[9] No longer do candidates have to campaign citywide trying to reach as many voters as possible; instead they target their energies on the district in which they are running. As a result, the campaigns can be more grassroots focused and less mass media oriented. Candidates do not need to be independently wealthy or necessarily seek the support of moneyed interests to compete. Lower cost campaigns should mean that more people are able to mount viable efforts to win local elective office. The logic of this argument is sound, but the evidence has not been compelling. For example, the Heilig and Mundt research looked for evidence that a district system holds down the influence of money on election results.[10] The results were mixed. In some of the cities they studied, average candidate spending decreased after a city moved to districts; in other cities, costs actually increased. Relatedly, in their study, Welch and Bledsoe concluded that, regardless of the electoral system used in a city, "The need for money screens out potential candidates."[11] However, these findings about the presence or absence of a district effect on campaign costs have become dated and their relevance to the situation in contemporary Austin is limited.

Campaign finance information reported by mayoral and council candidates in Austin for five different election cycles during the period from 2009 to 2016 reveals several patterns. As shown in Table 3.1, regardless of the election, winners on average spent more than losing candidates did, sometimes a lot more. This is not unusual. One of the persistent trends in American politics at every level is the influence of money on electoral success.[12] City elections in Austin do not buck this trend. Of course, other factors influence election outcomes and drive up costs, such as the presence of open seats in which there are no incumbents running and the use of runoff elections when no candidate in the general election receives a majority of the votes cast.

The data in Table 3.1 also reemphasize the aberrational nature of the 2014 election when all of the council seats and the mayor's post were on the ballot. With seventy-eight candidates, total election spending by candidates in excess of $5 million is not extreme, especially when one of the races is a citywide mayoral campaign. In fact, average campaign expenditures were lower in 2014 ($67,336) than they had been in the previous three elections. This suggests that at least one of the expectations of a district council—a lower cost of campaigning—was borne out. But average spending by winning candidates in 2014 ($208,381) was the highest of the five elections displayed in the table. Clearly, the average cost of winning a district council seat was greater than had it had been in earlier at-large elections. Relatedly, the change to districts stimulated more competition for council seats. An average of 7 candidates competed for each council seat in 2014 while in the 2011 council-only election, the average number of candidates per seat was 3.7. Given the dif- . ference of the average spending between all candidates and winning candi-

TABLE 3.1. CAMPAIGN FINANCE DATA

Election year and type	Candidates for mayor and city council					
	All candidates			Winning candidates		
	Total number of candidates on ballot	Total sum campaign expenditures* ($)	Mean campaign expenditures ($)	Number of winning candidates	Sum campaign expenditures ($)	Mean campaign expenditures ($)
2009 Mayor, council	12	1,429,716.68	119,143.06	5	906,242.50	181,248.50
2011 Council	11	916,265.78	83,296.89	3	553,989.77	184,663.26
2012 Mayor, council	14	1,049,007.84	74,929.13	4	756,096.84	189,024.21
2014 Mayor, council	78	5,252,244.27	67,336.47	11	2,292,185.65	208,380.51
2016 Council	14	1,130,335.29	80,738.24	5	685,333.92	137,066.78

Source: Office of the City Clerk, City of Austin, Campaign Finance Reports, various dates, available at http://www.austintexas.gov/department/campaign-finance-reports.

* Sums and means are expressed in current dollars. General elections and runoffs are included.

dates in 2014, it seems that many unsuccessful council candidates spent relatively little money in their campaigns.

Finally, taking a look at 2016 and the second set of district elections is instructive. That year, with five council seats up for election and all five incumbents seeking reelection, the average cost for all candidates increased over the 2014 figure. For winning candidates, though, the average cost dropped to $137,067, the lowest level of the five elections shown in Table 3.1. The degree of competition declined also, with an average of 2.8 candidates per seat, not surprising given the presence of an incumbent competing in every district. Three of the five incumbents were successful in their reelection bids. In the two districts in which a challenger beat an incumbent, the challengers' expenditures actually lagged the overall average expenditures for winning candidates for the 2016 council elections.

Of course, spending by candidates tells only part of the story. The *Austin Bulldog* reported that twenty-three political action committees (PACs) spent a total of $726,210 in the 2014 elections, led by the Austin Firefighters Association ($280,887) and the Austin Board of Realtors ($132,464).[13] The contributing PAC universe was relatively diverse including unions, business groups, partisan organizations, neighborhood groups, community associations, and single-issue groups. Their strategies for spending varied: some concentrated their contributions on a few candidates, while others hedged their bets and spread their funds more broadly. Many PACs waited until the field of candidates narrowed and spent more heavily in the runoff election cycle.

Council Diversity

The primary goal of AGR and their progressive supporters was to create an electoral system that would diversify the city council. By design, using a district system for council elections produces geographic diversity. Areas of Austin from which no council member had ever been elected were now represented by someone who lived in the area. In terms of race and ethnicity, the district lines generated the expected outcomes as well. Voters in the African American minority opportunity district elected an African American candidate; the three Hispanic opportunity districts elected Hispanic candidates. The results of the 2014 election provided several "I told you so" moments for AGR proponents. Austin's city council more closely resembled the racial and ethnic profile of the city, and, to a greater degree than ever before, descriptive representation had been achieved.

Moreover, district size and design led to ideological diversity on the council: three candidates with conservative credentials were elected, an infrequent occurrence in recent Austin city politics. The *Austin American-*

Statesman summed up the district effect this way: "The 10–1 system created a solidly Republican district in far Northwest Austin, a 50–50 district in Southwest Austin, and a Democrat-leaning but GOP-winnable district in West Austin."[14] Although their formal ties to the Republican Party varied, the newly elected council members from Districts 6, 8, and 10 were often referred to informally as "the three Republicans."

Women on the City Council

One other notable diversification of the city council arose from the 2014 district elections: a higher proportion of female candidates was elected. Of the ten district council members elected in 2014, seven were women. This result is somewhat at odds with the literature on local elections, which contends that women seem to fare better under an at-large election system.[15] In 1948, Emma Long was the first woman elected to the at-large city council in Austin, and she served for two decades, winning nine elections to the council and losing two. Three women were elected to the council in 1975, and the first female mayor of Austin was elected in 1977. Since then, the typical at-large Austin City Council had averaged two women among its membership.

Figure 3.1 tracks the trend in council membership (including the mayor) with regard to racial and ethnic minorities and women from 1971 to 2018. The trend line underscores the effect of the gentlemen's agreement. Over the forty-seven-year time frame, the Austin City Council consistently included two people of color. Until the 2014 election, the only deviations from that pattern occurred early in the period when only one person of color had been elected, and in 2001–2002 and 2005–2006 when the number of racial and ethnic minorities on the council reached three. For women, the pattern is more varied. Early on, there were no women on the Austin City Council; at other times women comprised just under one-third and, for a brief period, just over 40 percent of the council. But it was not until the 2014 election that the figure neared two-thirds of the council. Austin is out in front of most other U.S. cities in terms of gender diversity on the council. Contemporary research puts the average rate just under 23 percent.[16]

Having a majority female city council was a new situation for Austin and it led to an action by the city manager's office that raised more than a few eyebrows. Early in 2015, the city manager's office hired consultants from out of state to convene a training session for city staff who regularly interact with the city council on how to deal with a female-dominated governing body.[17] It might have seemed like a good idea to some, but the trainers' comments that, among other things, female council members prolong discussions by asking a lot questions and that they do not evince much interest in the cost

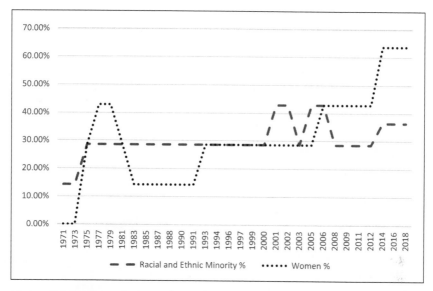

Figure 3.1. Racial, ethnic, and gender diversity on the Austin City Council, 1971–2018.

(Sources: Office of the City Clerk, City of Austin, Election History, accessed April 19–21, 2018, available at http://www.ci.austin.tx.us/election/search.cfm; Ken Martin, "Maps Prove a Select Few Govern Austin," *Austin Bulldog*, August 4, 2011, accessed March 14, 2018, available at https://www.theaustinbulldog.org/index.php?option=com_content&view=article&id=150:at-large-elections-favor-anglo-choices&catid=3:main-articles#comment-213.)

of city programs, rubbed many people the wrong way, including the female majority on the Austin City Council.[18] After council members learned that the session had occurred, they objected strenuously, and the video of the training session was removed from the city's website. It was not an optimal start, and it took time for the friction between some council members and the city manager's office to subside.

Occupational Diversity on the Council

Another aspect of diversity in representation is reflected in the occupation of city council members. One of the standard assumptions of moving from at-large to district systems is that more candidates of lower socioeconomic status will run for and win elective office. Both the Heilig and Mundt study and the Welch and Bledsoe research subjected this question to empirical testing. Using occupations as an indicator of status, Heilig and Mundt looked at a set of city councils that had switched from an at-large electoral system to a district-based system. The change to districts did not result in lower-status councils. Yes, there were fewer businesspersons on district councils than there had been on at-large councils where they had predominated, but more white-collar professionals served on district councils than on the earlier at-large councils. In general, although more blue-collar workers sought council office, they did not necessarily succeed in winning the office. Heilig and Mundt concluded that "voters in lower income and blue collar districts do not select council representatives from their social status."[19] However, the Welch and Bledsoe survey found modest support for the assumption about lower-status district councils when they compared council members elected at large to those elected from districts. The data showed proportionately fewer business owners and professionals among district council members while the percentage of blue-collar workers, although small, was higher in district councils than in at-large councils.[20]

What about Austin? Did the change to districts produce a more diverse city council in terms of occupation? Figure 3.2 provides a snapshot at three points in time. Not only is the comparison of occupations chronological; it also compares all candidates to winning candidates. Three points in time is in no way definitive but this short-term look provides an initial impression of a potential district effect. Candidates competing in the 2012 election ran at-large, while in the 2014 and 2016 elections, with the exception of the mayor, they ran in district races. Two points should be noted. First, the source for the occupation information is the ballot application filed by each candidate for city elective office. Therefore, the occupations are self-reported. Second, they were grouped by the author into twelve distinct occupational clusters that serve as the labels for the slices of the pie charts.[21]

The 2012 election saw candidates from seven different occupational fields compete for four seats (the mayor and three council places); in 2016 with five council seats in contention, the number of different occupational fields among the candidates was five. When the focus shifts to the winners, the occupational diversity narrows considerably. In 2012, all four of the positions were won by incumbents, three of whom listed their occupations as elected officials, the fourth incumbent described his occupation as education, which creates the one dissimilar slice in the 2012 winning candidates' pie chart. In 2016, the pattern was similar to 2012: the majority of the winners were from the category of government/elected officials, as three of five incumbents won reelection. The other winners included one candidate from the science/engineering category and one from a nonprofit/community organization.

The election of 2014 tends to disrupt any incipient patterns from the 2012 and 2016 data with seventy-eight candidates competing for eleven positions. In that election, the number of occupations in the candidate pool was large: twelve different fields, with the business/finance sector comprising the largest slice (23 percent). The occupational data also indicate that several candi-

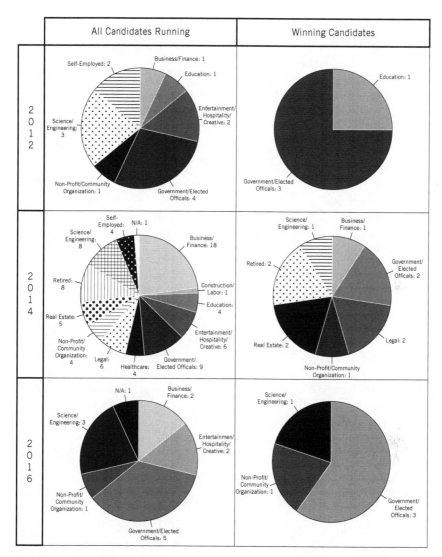

Figure. 3.2. Occupations of city council candidates and winners, in 2012, 2014, and 2016.

(Source: Office of the City Clerk, City of Austin, Texas, Ballot Applications, accessed May 6–8, 2018, available at http://www.austintexas.gov/content/2012-ballot-applications; http://austintexas.gov/cityclerk/elections/ballotapplications2014.htm; http://www.austintexas.gov/content/ballotapplications-2016.)

dates working in entertainment, hospitality, and/or creative fields filed for election in 2014 and 2016. Although the occupational diversity diminishes when the focus shifts to winners, it remains more varied than it was in either 2012 or 2016. There was no dominant occupational cluster among the eleven winners: two government/elected officials, two in real estate, two from the legal community, two retirees, one from business/finance, one from science/engineering, and one from the nonprofit/community organization sector. But with seven occupational fields represented, by any measure, the new, larger Austin council was diverse in terms of career paths and employment. Still, despite the range of occupations, council winners were employed in professional endeavors, none of them were blue-collar workers or engaged in lower-status occupations.[22] Even so, their incomes varied widely, according to council members' financial disclosure statements reviewed by the *Austin Bulldog*.[23]

Council Conflict and the Development of Coalitions

At-large councils have been faulted for operating in a kind of "groupthink" mode, with high levels of consensus.[24] After all, the city as a whole is the constituency for each council member, so that fact alone portends greater agreement among them.[25] In their study, Heilig and Mundt hypothesized that, compared to an at-large council, the proceedings of district councils would be characterized by "greater and more overt controversy, indicated by increased proportions of non-unanimous votes and by increased disagreement in council discussions."[26] However, with regard to conflict, only one-third of the cities they studied showed the predicted pattern of increased conflict and less unanimity; for the other cities the pattern was more mixed. Yet a different trend was found in the council members surveyed by Welch and Bledsoe. District council members reported higher levels of factionalism and lower levels of unanimity within their councils than at-large council members did.[27] Heilig and Mundt also expected district councils to develop "voting coalitions based on race, ethnicity, and district demographics."[28] Here, the preponderance of evidence was somewhat stronger. The development of coalitions and the emergence of bloc voting was found in some of the councils in their study especially immediately after the change to districts. Much of this behavior within the council appeared to be dependent on high levels of cohesion within the previously underrepresented groups.

In Austin, expectations were high that a geographically based council would bring a diversity of perspectives and preferences to the council. As a consequence, the level of unanimity in council voting was expected to decline from the predistrict at-large era. Table 3.2 compares the voting patterns of the

TABLE 3.2. CITY COUNCIL VOTING PATTERNS, 2012–2017

Year	Council type	Total votes taken*	Number of unanimous votes†	Unanimous votes (%)
2012	At large	1,399	1,321	94.4
2013	At large	1,863	1,707	91.6
2014	At large	2,046	1,897	92.7
2015	District	1,293	1,042	80.6
2016	District	1,410	1,102	78.2
2017	District	1,315	1,110	84.4

Source: City of Austin, City Council, various dates, available at https://www.austintexas.gov/department/city-council/archive/city_council_meeting_archives.htm.

* Vote totals include council votes on motions, ordinances, and resolutions by city council members at council meetings.

† A unanimous vote is one in which there are zero votes against the motion, ordinance, or resolution.

city council during a six-year period, with three at-large councils and three district councils. A unanimous vote is defined as one in which no council member votes against a motion, ordinance, or resolution. Without exception, the levels of unanimity were higher in at-large councils than in district councils. The 2012 at-large council is notable for the degree of unanimity (94.4 percent); the 2016 district council recorded the lowest level (78.2 percent). Still, it is important to acknowledge that although unanimity has declined, experience with a district-based council is fairly brief and this may not be a perpetual trend. And, of course, along with the adoption of districts, the size of the city council increased, making unanimity more difficult to achieve irrespective of the electoral system. Moreover, even at its lowest point, more than three-quarters of the votes taken by the district council had no council members voting in opposition. In general, the level of disagreement on the Austin City Council is greater than it was in recent at-large councils, still one cannot conclude that the district councils have been riven with dissent and disagreement.

Close observers of the Austin City Council suggest that, on occasion, logrolling or vote trading takes place within the council.[29] Sometimes, it is an explicit arrangement: council member A agrees to support council member B's proposal in exchange for council member B's support of a proposal that council member A intends to make. Other times, it is more a matter of deference: council member A votes with council member B because the issue is noncontroversial and affects only council member B's district.[30] The prevalence of these differently motivated logrolling behaviors is murky because council members do not acknowledge these actions publicly. Still, it is not uncommon to find instances of logrolling in many legislative bodies. In fact, one of the objections to district-based electoral systems is that by virtue of their design, they encourage logrolling and vote trading.[31] Taking a different tack, others have contended that logrolling actually generates efficiencies in legislative decision-making.[32]

There did not seem to be any sharp cleavages within the Austin City Council during the first three years of a district electoral system. For instance, council members representing the minority opportunity districts did not necessarily vote the same way on issues while the remainder of the council voted the other way. However, an analysis of voting at regular and special-called meetings, since the advent of districts, showed the existence of several pairings within the council that may reflect the existence of underlying, but thus far inchoate, coalitions. These occurred between the council member in District 2 and the member in District 5, between council members in District 7 and District 9, and between the member in District 3 and the mayor. In other words, the voting behavior of the council member from District 2 most often mirrored that of the council member from District 5 and vice versa; similar congruence was found for Districts 7 and 9, and District 3 and the mayor. These general patterns were confirmed by a more focused analysis of 316 council votes on "high-interest issues" as defined by the *Austin American-Statesman* from 2015 through the first quarter of 2018.[33] The three pairs of council members identified above had the highest rates of agreement in their votes on these issues.

A Shift in the Agenda?

At-large and district councils may diverge in the topics they address. Obviously, the problem of the counterfactual exists, that is, one does not know what an at-large city council would have done in Austin had the electoral system not changed. Perhaps a council elected citywide would have pursued the same issues in the same way as the district council has done. We simply cannot know. But we can compare how the focus of the district council differs from that of an at-large council at an earlier point in time. This is not an ideal comparison because the context is different, but it does offer a glimpse of a potential shift in the council's substantive agenda. Previous research attempting to capture the substantive impact of the change from citywide elections to district elections grappled with the same dilemma. For example, Heilig and Mundt found some modest changes in council policy focus after districts were instituted but far short of "dramatic changes in the distribution of policy benefits."[34] Within district councils, they found that greater attention was paid to where new city-funded facilities would be placed, a predictable consequence of a council elected by a geographically determined constituency.[35] Allocational decisions clearly matter to district council members.[36]

To gauge the policy and issue agenda in Austin, ten topics were identified that are regularly cited in public opinion polling as being of interest to city residents.[37] Using those topics as keywords, council agendas from regular and special-called meetings were searched to produce a frequency tally reflecting the final four years of the at-large council and the first four years of the district council. The tallies and the percentage change over time appear in Table 3.3. As is readily apparent, substantial changes occur from one time period to the next. For example, although the keyword "development" appears with the greatest regularity in both time periods, its occurrence as an agenda item decreases 17 percent with the advent of districts.[38] Other issues experience even greater declines in the district era: environment, arts, and technology drop by more than 30 percent. Getting more attention from the district council are topics such as affordable/affordability (with a 225 percent increase in agenda mentions), historic preservation (up 140 percent), and housing (up 91 percent). To some extent, these are topics that political scientist Mirya Holman considers "urban women's issues," and one should expect them to appear more frequently on the council agenda as the number of women on a council increases. Regardless of the electoral system used to select the council, it is likely that the focus of a city council will vary from one period to the next as new issues emerge and others recede. But the magnitude of the changes reported in Austin suggests a shift in emphasis once a district system was in place.

TABLE 3.3. COUNCIL AGENDA ITEMS			
Keyword*	Number of agenda item mentions, 2011–2014*	Number of agenda item mentions, 2015–2018*	Change (%)
Affordable/affordability	85	276	225
Arts	149	98	−34
Budget	599	441	−26
Development	1,016	842	−17
Downtown	171	123	−28
Environment	125	59	−53
Historic preservation	20	48	140
Housing	270	515	91
Technology	88	57	−35
Transportation/mobility	258	335	30

Source: City of Austin, Historical Agenda Items (2004–2018), various dates, available at https://data.austintexas.gov/City-Government/Historical-Agenda-Item-Dataset-2004-2018-/akgy-tbxy.

* The number reflects agenda items featuring the keyword in the item description for city council/committee meetings during the time period.

Council Operations

The 2014 city council was largely a group of novices, with only one member who had served on the previous council as well as another council member who had served one term in the state legislature. The mayor was new to the council, surviving a general election that included two former council members among the candidates. Yet, what this group lacked in council service was countered by, in most instances, longtime involvement in community affairs and an avowed commitment to representing their constituents. Once inaugurated, the first order of business for the new council was orientation, which was a three-day event intended to acquaint council members with the structure and operation of city government and the key players and their responsibilities. Subsequently, the council embarked upon a series of workshops that involved two-hour deep dives into twenty-four policy areas such as comprehensive planning, watershed protection, resource recovery, neighborhood issues, and public safety.[39]

Committee Structure and Council Outreach

Next up on the council's to-do list was its own operation, in particular, its use of an expanded and more deliberative structure in which committees would review proposed ordinances before they reached the full council. The stated goals of the new design were more efficiency and greater transparency, along with a more effective process for public input.[40] Austin City Council meetings were well known for lasting, on occasion, well into the late evening, frustrating both council members and constituents in attendance. Proposed was a thirteen-committee structure, later amended to ten committees. The ordinance the council adopted laid out specific committee guidelines, including committee size and function, staffing, decision-making process, and rules for citizen participation in committee hearings.[41] Two years later, amid concerns that the work of some committees overlapped and sometimes duplicated what was being done by the city's numerous boards and commissions, the council reduced the number of committees to five: Audit and Finance, Mobility, Austin Energy Utility Oversight, Health and Human Services, and Housing and Planning.[42] Lengthy council meetings continue to occur as members deliberate more thoroughly than the at-large council typically did, according to longtime council observers.[43]

Another noticeable change once the district council was in place was a demonstrated increase in the outreach activities undertaken by council members. The commitment to increasing citizen involvement was signaled by the creation of a Task Force on Civic Engagement and the scheduling of a spate of town hall meetings in districts throughout the city.[44] Compared to the at-large council, Austin's new council embraced more of an ombudsman role, a behavior in line with earlier research on district council roles.[45] Current council members reported an uptick in constituent contacts as a result of these outreach efforts. Some of the contacting has a narrow focus such as complaints about illegally parked cars in residential areas or disputes between neighbors. Regardless, in the view of local officials, the district system has strengthened the connection between constituents and council members.[46] And Austinites seem to like the increased interaction, at least insofar as results from an informal and nonscientific poll conducted by the *Austin American-Statesman* can be relied on.[47] One year after the district council took office, respondents gave high marks to council members for being responsive to constituents; in fact, "responsive" may have been the modal word among the comments posted by the *Statesman*.

The Council-City Manager Relationship

The relationship between the city council and the city manager is important, and it can be problematic in any community. As discussed in Chapter 1, in the council-manager form of government, the council sets the policy direction for the city and the city manager and city staff implement that direction. In practice, though, the distinction between what the council does and what the manager does is not so precise. This is especially true when a veteran city manager is working with a new council, which was the situation in Austin in 2015 when the district council took office. The city manager, Marc Ott, had been Austin's city manager since 2008 and had been dubbed "the most powerful man at City Hall" in the local press.[48] The change in council structure was said to give Ott "11 bosses rather than seven" and at least some of those new bosses had been critical during the campaign of Ott's performance as manager.[49] The relationship between the manager and the council had its difficult moments over the first year and a half but in June 2016, the council voted 7–1 with 3 abstentions, to give him a 7.6 percent pay raise. Two months later, Ott announced that he was resigning his position in Austin to become executive director of the International City/County Management Association in Washington, DC. It is unclear whether the change in the council had any impact on Ott's decision to leave Austin, but his departure meant that the district council could handpick his replacement.[50]

After a national search, in February 2018, the council voted unanimously to hire as the new city manager, Spencer Cronk, who had been city coordinator (similar to a chief administrator) for the city of Minneapolis. Prior to his position in Minneapolis, Cronk had served as commissioner of the Minnesota Department of Administration and had worked in New York City mayor Michael Bloomberg's administration. Given Cronk's employment history, the general impression among council watchers was that as a non-traditional city manager, he would exhibit more of a collaborative leadership style.[51] In the view of some council members, high-level city staff had become a bit too independent of the city council. The district-based council made it clear that it intended to carve out a more active role for itself and sought a city manager attuned to that approach.[52] One city council member commented that Cronk's appeal lay in his "emphasis on prevention, his emphasis on tearing down silos, and his . . . fresh perspective."[53]

Within four months of taking office, Cronk announced that he was reorganizing the top leadership structure in the city manager's office and reorienting his executive team toward city council–endorsed goals, namely economic opportunity and affordability, health and environment, safety and mobility, culture and lifelong learning, and a government that works.[54] In another move reflecting a new direction, he presented the proposed fiscal year (FY) 2019 city budget to the council and the public in a special-called meeting at Austin's Mexican American Cultural Center. "I want people to understand these changes," he said, "and I'm simply making it more in line with transparency and openness—getting out of City Hall and out into the community."[55]

The adoption of a district system represented a paradigm shift of sorts for city staff, particularly in how they present information to the council. Council members who represent districts are interested in district-level data, for example, knowing in which districts capital improvement projects are being undertaken. Neighborhood associations, which have maintained strong ties to their council members, are also attentive to the geographic distribution and spatial impacts of city actions. Initially, there was some pushback regarding disaggregation of information to the district level, but, eventually, presenting certain information in a more granular format became standard operating procedure for staff. That said, the council, too, has received criticism from those who say that council deliberations too often veer into the weeds rather than staying at a higher plane focused on the big picture.[56]

Council Costs

Increasing the size of the council by four members has had budget consequences. Prior to the adoption of the 10–1 plan, city staff had estimated the annual fiscal impact of additional council members and staff to be approximately $1,396,000 annually.[57] This total assumes a cost of $349,000 for each new council office and was based on the budget for an at-large council office, which in FY 2013–2014 was $328,305. These estimates have proved to be low. For FY 2015–2016, the budget for each council office was $437,778; for FY 2016–2017, it was $442,764. Any money left over in a council office budget at the end of a fiscal year can be carried over or reallocated to various initiatives. In fact, at the first regular meeting of the district council in 2015, a resolution was adopted giving council members the authority to forgo their salaries if they chose to and reallocate the funds to other areas within their office budgets.[58] For the record, as of fiscal year 2016–2017, the mayor's salary was $82,387 annually, council member salaries were $74,235 annually. Table 3.4 displays budget information for six fiscal years.

Adopting a district system, irrespective of the size of the council, has contributed to increased council costs. After a year of using the same staffing ratio as the at-large council (four full-time equivalents [FTEs] in each office), council members made the case for more staff support. The mayor, although elected citywide as in the past, was the first to propose an increase in staffing, requesting to nearly double the size of his office staff. Subsequently, the mayor's proposal was scaled back to three new staff positions and became part of a recommendation to add one more staff position to each council member's office. This meant thirteen new positions at a total annual cost of nearly $1 million.[59] The argument supporting the staff increase boiled down to an insufficient capacity to meet the demands of a council emphasizing constituent work and a more time-intensive operational structure. The

TABLE 3.4. MAYOR AND CITY COUNCIL APPROVED BUDGETS, VARIOUS FISCAL YEARS*

Fiscal year	Total amount budgeted, Mayor and Council Department† ($)	Mayor's office ($)	Number of FTEs	Each city council office ($)	Number of FTEs
2012–2013	2,507,598	503,549	6	321,062	4
2013–2014	2,571,423	512,552	6	328,305	4
2014–2015	4,186,166	524,546	6	346,184	4
2015–2016	5,156,634	841,721	9	437,778	5
2016–2017	5,758,383	850,910	9	442,764	5
2017–2018	6,221,060	901,874	9	467,052	5

Source: City of Austin, Austin Finance Online, various dates, available at https://www.austintexas.gov/financeonline/afo_content.cfm?s=1&p=57.

* Approved budget amounts may be amended. Actual budgets for council offices may vary due to carryover funds.

† Total amount budgeted for the Mayor and Council Department includes shared administrative costs not allocated to specific offices within the department.

amended proposal was adopted and beginning with FY 2015–2016, the mayor's office was budgeted for nine FTE positions (this figure includes the mayor) and each council office was budgeted for five FTEs (which includes the council member). Did changing the electoral structure in Austin (and enlarging the size of the council) increase the costs of operating the mayor and council department? The answer is an unequivocal "yes." The amount budgeted in the last fiscal year of an at-large council was $2,571,423; in FY 2016–2017, the figure was $5,758,383. Converting these current dollar amounts to constant dollars shows the increase in costs to be approximately $2 million, in round figures.

Evaluations of Council Performance

The type of electoral system change experienced in Austin was a long time coming. The mobilization of the community in support of adopting districts, be it the 10–1 plan or the alternative 8–2–1 plan, was significant. Once districts were in place, opinion polls sought to gauge the public's feeling about the new system. In a 2015 Voices of the Austin Community poll, respondents were asked about their level of optimism/pessimism about "the new 10–1 City Council structure."[60] The assessments of residents polled were mostly positive: 40 percent said they were optimistic, and only 22 percent were pessimistic. One-third were more circumspect, indicating that they were either unfamiliar with the new 10–1 structure or undecided about it. The same poll conducted in 2017 asked whether respondents thought that the change to districts "has made city government in Austin better or worse."[61] Nearly twice as many Austinites said "better" (34 percent) than "worse" (18 percent) but nearly half reserved judgment saying they did not have a strong opinion or did not know enough. These results do not radiate unvarnished enthusiasm for the change in the electoral system, but neither do they convey dismay over the change.

The *Austin American-Statesman* weighed in on council performance as the first year of the district system drew to a close and assessed it as, on balance, so-so.[62] On the plus side, there had been no descent into ward politics as some had feared, where council members' attention to district-specific issues would become detrimental to citywide priorities. But, less positively, neither was there significant progress on addressing some of the city's major challenges such as a high cost of living and unrelenting traffic congestion. Similarly, when the city conducted its annual community survey in 2018, "traffic flow on major city streets" was one issue on which Austin fared poorly. However, in general, the public's assessment of city services was positive: Nearly two-thirds of those surveyed reported being either "satisfied" or "very satisfied" with the overall quality of city services.[63] Showing a notable increase over the previous year was the public's satisfaction with city efforts to promote and assist small, minority, and/or women-owned businesses, which increased by 10 percent.

Council Elections after 2014

To achieve a staggered election schedule as set out in the revised city charter, five of the district council members elected in 2014 served a two-year term. All five incumbents sought reelection in 2016, and three of them were successful, winning with 60 percent or more of the vote in the general election: Greg Casar (District 4), Delia Garza (District 2), and Leslie Pool (District 7). One of the incumbents who was defeated, Don Zimmermann, was considered the most conservative member of the council elected in 2014, and, during his two-year term, he was more likely than other council members to be on the losing side of council votes. He was defeated for the District 6 seat by the candidate he had beaten 51 percent to 49 percent in a 2014 runoff election, Jimmy Flannigan. In the 2016 rematch, Flannigan received 56 percent of the vote, Zimmerman 44 percent. The other incumbent loss came in District 10, where Sheri Gallo was unseated in a runoff election by Alison Alter, 64 percent to 36 percent. Council member Gallo was one of the so-called three Republicans on the council, even though her affiliation with the GOP was somewhat episodic. One of the pivotal issues in District 10, which has the highest median household income of the council districts, was the pace of new development.[64]

Emblematic of the impact of scheduling city elections to coincide with elections for higher office, the 2016 election with a presidential race at the top of the ballot drew 64.6 percent of Austin's registered voters to the polls.[65] Undoubtedly, some voter roll-off occurred, that is, not all of them voted in the council election. In the five districts with council races, turnout rates ranged from 37 percent in District 2 to 54.9 percent in District 10.[66] Only the council election in District 10 remained unresolved after the general election, and a runoff election was held in December 2016 in which nearly one-quarter of the district's electorate participated.

In sum, the 2016 elections resulted in a more left-leaning city council, one in which the already limited impact of council conservatives was further reduced. As the new council members on the dais, Alter and Flannigan quickly embraced an activist, and sometimes independent, role for themselves.[67]

The remaining council seats, including the mayor's, were on the ballot in 2018. Although in 2016 all of the two-year term council incumbents had sought reelection, this was not the case with the four-year term council members. Two of them decided that one term was enough: Ora Houston in District 1 and Ellen Troxclair in District 8 chose not to seek reelection. One factor contributing to council member Troxclair's decision was that she had become the lone conservative on the council, owing to the defeats of Zimmermann and Gallo in 2016. A different situation developed in District 5 when the incumbent council member, Ann Kitchens, a former state representative, drew no opposition and was assured of another term.

Twenty-nine candidates competed for the six seats. With 58.1 percent of registered voters participating in the election, the incumbent mayor, Steve Adler, squared off against six challengers and won easily without a runoff.[68] The four contested council seats attracted between four and seven competitors; incumbents fared better than they had in 2016. Kathie Tovo, the only council member who had also served on the at-large council, was reelected in District 9. Incumbent Sabino Renteria won in District 3, besting his sister in a runoff election. Both of the races without incumbents competing were decided in runoff elections in which far fewer voters participated. In District 1, with 56.3 percent of registered voters in the district participating, the two top candidates finished the election with fewer than two hundred votes separating them. In the runoff with a voter turnout rate of 8.9 percent, an African American candidate, Natasha Harper-Madison, beat her Hispanic challenger by a wide margin. In District 8, newcomer Paige Ellis, an environmental consultant, defeated her conservative opponent to cement what the *Austin Business Journal* termed "a liberal monopoly on the council."[69] The level of voter participation declined by 65 percent between the general election and the runoff. The 2018 elections did not result in changes to the racial, ethnic, or gender composition of the council.

This being Austin, the 2018 ballot also featured eleven propositions, most of which were bond measures. All of the bond issues passed easily including a $250 million bond issue for affordable housing, one of the signature issues of the district council. Two citizen initiative propositions sought to rein in the council: one would have slowed the process for revising the city's land development code; the other would have required an efficiency study of the city's operations. Both of these measures were defeated. But they gave rise to a growing lament from some council members, and especially the mayor, that the petition signature threshold in the Austin city charter was too low, thereby making ballot access too easy to achieve.[70] Ironically, even as the mayor was making the case, a well-funded group of neighborhood activists was gathering signatures for a ballot initiative that, had it been approved, would have blocked the deal the city had entered into for the construction of a stadium for a new Major League Soccer franchise.

After the swearing-in ceremonies for the newly elected council members in 2019, Mayor Adler voiced a note of optimism about the city's future, vowing "to move our city forward in a way that is inclusive, innovative and intentionally improvisational."[71] District 2 council member Delia Garza, who was selected by her colleagues to serve as mayor pro tem, declared a similar objective. "I think this is an opportunity to really move the needle on how we manage growth and do it in a progressive way. I think this City Council will be one of the most progressive in terms of understanding the need to plan and manage our growth, and that we're no longer a little college town. . . . We're a big city, and if we don't plan for that, we're hurting our most vulnerable."[72] The consequences of growth will continue to challenge the city: In 2019, for the third consecutive year, the publication *U.S. News and World Report* ranked Austin as "the best place to live in America."[73]

CONCLUSION

Looking below the Surface . . . and Forward

F our decades is a long time for an idea to move from the proposal stage to adoption and implementation. In any city, forty years would be a long time to wait for district elections, especially when other big cities in the same state are replacing their at-large systems with districts and when the failure to do so leads to federal lawsuits. In Austin, a city that prides itself on its progressivism, a forty-year wait is especially perplexing. Austin is typically a city on the cutting edge, not trailing behind. On an issue such as the legitimate representation of racial and ethnic minority group interests, Austin should have been among the leaders, but it was not. Now, as Austin's district-based city council deals with a thicket of challenging issues, new voices and perspectives are being heard.

A Brief Summary

From a rocky beginning, Austin has endured to become the country's eleventh largest city, one that is celebrated for its natural beauty, its vibrant economy, its cultural richness, and, yes, its weirdness. It is a Sunbelt success story. The city council has been involved at every step of the city's development, sometimes leading, sometimes following, but involved nonetheless. As explained in Chapter 1, Austin has adjusted its governmental form numerous times to meet changing circumstances, and the issue of representation was ever present but seldom at the forefront. The heart of the representation question was, as it still is, the responsiveness of the city council to varied interests and preferences in the community. At-large and district electoral systems have been shown to advantage different segments of the population when it comes to winning council seats and enacting public policies.[1] In terms of growth and development, the at-large system had worked well for the city, but it performed less effectively in dealing with the consequences of Austin's economic success. The interests of many groups of people and many parts of the city were being bypassed or overrun in the meantime. In the early twenty-first century, the issue of representation could not be sidestepped much longer.

The story of the twists and turns in Austin's march, or, more accurately, its slow but persistent slog, to geographically based, single-member city council districts is the focus of Chapter 2. Austin's voters formally took up the district question on six different occasions beginning in 1973 and turned it down each time. The reasons differed: sometimes defeat was related to the design of the district proposal, sometimes it could be attributed to the concerted opposition of those benefiting from the status quo, and at other times it was more of a matter of intervening events. In many instances it seemed as if most voters were simply not engaged in the issue. But, in 2012, the outcome was different largely due to the efforts of AGR, a seemingly indefatigable grassroots organization that designed a smart campaign to secure passage of an initiative proposition on districts. Fairness was at the core of AGR's message to Austin residents; its organizational dynamic was fueled by a streak of populism. When Austin voters went to the polls in November 2012, they approved the district proposition; actually, they approved two district propositions. As a result, representation was about to change; the only question was the extent of the change.

Chapter 3 explores the changes that have occurred with the adoption of a district electoral system. Several outcomes are identified, but it is important to remember that districts were not the only change approved by the voters in 2012: the size of the council also increased from seven to eleven members. The first district elections in 2014 produced a record number of candidates and generated a change in descriptive representation, particularly with regard to race, ethnicity, and gender. There is some evidence of a change in emphasis in the substantive agenda of the council, although it cannot be said that these changes are solely the result of the district system. But it is apparent that new perspectives are being heard. The new council adjusted aspects of its internal operations, increased its own staff, and modified its relationship with the city manager's office. Notably, council members pursued more constituent service and community engagement. Concerns that the district council would devolve into ward politics appear to have been unfounded thus far.[2] Initial evaluations of the district council's performance have tended to be encouraging although not glowing. Perhaps reflective of that sentiment, when five incumbent council members sought reelection in 2016, three were reelected, and two were defeated. In the 2018 council elections, two incumbents chose not to run for another term, but the four (including the mayor) who did were reelected. Within four years, four of the first set of district council members were no longer on the dais.

On the Horizon

What of the future? What will the city's next decade or two be like? Austin has been remarkably successful over the past thirty years, according to most metrics used to gauge city success. But amid the indicators of success, some discontent is evident. Austin can be a contentious place at times, with much debate over issues and directions, and the district electoral system institutionalizes this condition. In many ways, this is good. Residents care about their city and do not want to see it change . . . or they care about their city, but they do want to see it change. Two issues offer some insights into the challenges facing the city council: creating an effectively functioning city government and revising the city's land development code. Moreover, both of the issues intersect—the first indirectly, the second directly—with Austin's contextual conditions: its creative city status, the recurring tensions among developers, environmentalists, and neighborhoods, and the contested vision for the city's future.

A Government That Works

One of the goals set out by the district-based city council is creating "a government that works," but progress toward this goal is disputed. As noted in Chapter 3, the new city manager hired by the council revamped his leadership team in 2018, organizing it around the council's five overarching priorities. This seems a logical first step in explicitly connecting city operations to the espoused goals. A second step is the development of performance measures that align the work of city offices with the priorities. However, some segments of the community are not convinced that Austin city government is functioning efficiently. A curious coalition of individuals and groups, some that lean conservative/libertarian and others that tend to be progressive, pushed for an audit of government efficiency at city hall.[3] Taking a page from AGR's playbook, Citizens for an Accountable Austin (CAA) launched a petition drive that was successful in placing the question of an independent audit before the voters at the November 2018 election.

Promoters of the independent audit, the cost of which could reach several million dollars to execute, contended that the city would save substantially more than that once inefficiencies were eliminated, although widely divergent cost estimates and potential savings figures abounded.[4] Opponents of the audit argued that it was unnecessary because the city regularly conducts audits of its operations; moreover, they raised questions about CAA's sources of funding.[5] The matter bogged down over ballot language, with proponents preferring a simple statement: "Shall a city ordinance be adopted requiring a comprehensive, independent third-party efficiency audit of all city operations and budget?"[6] City officials, on the other hand, wanted a ballot question that explained the role of the city auditing office that regularly conducts audits of city departments and spending and publishes the results.[7] They settled on this language: "Without using the existing internal City Auditor or existing independent external auditor, shall the City Code be amended to require an efficiency study of the City's operational and fiscal performance performed by a third-party audit consultant, at an estimated cost of $1 million–$5 million?"[8] Lawsuits were filed over the wording of the ballot question, and the Texas Supreme Court decided in favor of the city's ballot language. As noted in Chapter 3, voters rejected the proposition but the forces promoting the efficiency audit remain active watchdogs of what goes on at city hall.

Rewriting the Land Development Code

Austin's status as a creative city, the ongoing conflicts among developers, environmentalists, and neighborhoods, and contested visions of what Austin should become are important factors in understanding the city's entanglement in efforts to overhaul its land development code. Imagine Austin, the city's comprehensive plan, approved in 2012, called for a rewrite of the land development code, which had not been thoroughly updated since 1984.[9] The code dictates what can be built where, and, once adopted, it establishes the city's physical form for the next twenty to thirty years. As has been said, "When it comes to City Hall politics, there's land use, and then there's everything else."[10] The city spent six years and approximately $8 million working with consultants to rewrite the city's outdated land development code, aiming to reconcile it with principles laid out in Imagine Austin.

The 1,600-page rewrite, called CodeNEXT, quickly became dubbed "CodeNEVER" upon the release of drafts in 2017. A poll commissioned by the Greater Austin Chamber of Commerce showed that public enthusiasm for CodeNEXT was negatively correlated with length of residency.[11] Among those living in Austin for less than a decade, support for the rewrite was 63 percent; however, it was only 27 percent for longtime resident Austinites of thirty-five years or more. The objections were numerous and varied, but they mostly boiled down to this: some in the city demanded more neighborhood preservation, while others called for increased housing density. In short, it was neighborhood preservationists versus prodensity urbanists. As council discussion of CodeNEXT progressed, yard signs popped up throughout the city, "CodeNEXT Wrecks Austin," was one popular sentiment, as was "Kill CodeNEXT." Even the city's Zoning and Platting Commission voted to end the CodeNEXT process. Anti-CodeNEXT groups filed lawsuits against the city, and before long an exasperated city council voted unanimously to abandon CodeNEXT. With the problems that CodeNEXT was supposed to address—traffic congestion, soaring housing costs, and intense gentrification, to name a few—still looming, the council asked the city manager to come up with another approach. As with so many things, the devil will be in the details of any proposed solution. In the meantime, voters defeated a citizen-initiated proposition in 2018 to make it more difficult for the city to rewrite its land development code in the future. The land development issue, with its consequences for affordability, gentrification, and neighborhood preservation, is one that roils Austin's progressives and can split them into warring camps.

Redefining "Progressive"?

The appeal of creative cities often generates consequences for the community such as income inequality, displacement, and unaffordable housing. Austin is a living laboratory for these consequences. On Richard Florida's "new urban crisis" index, published in 2017, Austin ranked ninth among large metropolitan areas, a top-ten ranking that the city does not welcome.[12] The challenge for the city council is to address these consequences effectively, but, as the brouhaha over CodeNEXT has shown, this is not easy to do. Since the 1970s, Austin has been able to fashion solutions that allow competing interests to achieve part of their vision of the future. None of the involved parties achieved its most preferred outcome but each was able to salvage a sufficiently satisfactory result. These negotiated solutions may have been optimal solutions for Austin as a whole, but their continued viability seems in jeopardy as the vision for the city becomes even more contested.

It is as yet uncertain whether a district-based council can serve as a solution, uniting disparate parts of the city. Generally, widespread concurrence exists on progressive values such as social equity. It is not surprising that in 2018, Austin was the first Texas city to pass an expansive mandatory paid sick leave policy covering the entire private sector, with some variation in the requirements based on the size of the firm.[13] Moreover, as the proverbial blueberry in the tomato soup, Austin filed a lawsuit against the state's 2017 anti–sanctuary city law and declared itself a "freedom city," restricting police attempts to question immigrants about their status and cutting back on arrests of immigrants for nonviolent crimes.[14] In 2019, Austin formally endorsed the progressive "Green New Deal" concept for addressing economic inequality and climate change. Except in the more conservative corners of Austin, agreement can be reached on these matters. But, as we have seen, issues such as land development have become thornier and more divisive.

The district system has been successful in bringing representation to more people and more parts of the city. As a result, more voices are being heard. For example, the ongoing redevelopment of Austin's east side, which is producing significant gentrification and displacing some longtime residents many of whom are African American or Hispanic, is not being treated as an inevitable by-product of growth. It is now an issue that is front and center on the council's agenda, put there largely because of the efforts of city council members representing East Austin neighborhoods. The council responded by including a $250 million affordable housing package as part of $925 million in bond issues that voters approved in November 2018, by far the largest affordable housing effort that Austin had ever attempted.[15]

Some urbanists have argued that America is on the cusp of a period of "new localism" and that it is at the local level of government where contemporary problems will be solved with ingenuity and innovative practices.[16] The greatly advantaged city of Austin offers a compelling test of that conjecture. In 1983, at the start of Austin's economic boom, a *New York Times* story featured the headline, "Booming Austin Fears It Will Lose Its Charms."[17] In the ensuing thirty-six years, this question has not lost its potency.[18] The at-large council was able to serve the interests of liberal Austin as a whole, but it was less responsive to the concerns of residents in certain parts of the city. The Austin City Council is now composed of individuals elected by voters in ten geographic districts who represent the interests of specific constituencies. Given the council's composition and its commitment to doing things differently, Austin may be on its way to redefining what it means to be a "progressive" city.

NOTES

INTRODUCTION

1. With a 2017 population estimated at 950,715, Austin is the fourth largest city in Texas, in between Dallas (1,341,075) and Fort Worth (874,168). It is the eleventh largest city in the United States. See the U.S. Census Bureau, "Census Bureau Reveals Fastest-Growing Large Cities," May 24, 2018, available at https://census.gov/newsroom/press-releases/2018/estimates-cities.html#table3.

2. City of Austin, Imagine Austin, accessed August 22, 2018, available at https://www.austintexas.gov/imagineaustin.

3. Anthony M. Orum, *Power, Money and the People* (Austin: Texas Monthly Press, 1987).

4. Carl Grodach, "Before and after the Creative City: The Politics of Urban Cultural Policy in Austin, Texas," *Journal of Urban Affairs* 34, no. 1 (2012): 81–97.

5. Sandra Zaragoza, "Q&A: Creative Class Author on Austin," *Austin Business Journal*, November 22, 2010, available at https://www.bizjournals.com/austin/blog/creative/2010/11/qa-creative-class-author-on-austin.html.

6. Jimmy Im, "These Are the 10 Best Places to Live in the US in 2019," *CNBC.com*, April 15, 2019, available at https://www.cnbc.com/2019/04/15/us-news-world-report-best-places-to-live-in-the-us-in-2019.html.

7. Paul G. Lewis and Max Neiman, *Custodians of Place: Governing the Growth and Development of Cities* (Washington, DC: Georgetown University Press, 2009).

8. Chris Tausanovitch and Christopher Warshaw, "Measuring Constituent Policy Preferences in Congress, State Legislatures, and Cities," *Journal of Politics* 75, no. 2 (April 2013): 330–342.

9. Joshua Long, *Weird City: Sense of Place and Creative Resistance in Austin, Texas* (Austin: University of Texas Press, 2010), 20.

10. William Scott Swearingen Jr. *Environmental City: People, Place, Politics, and the Meaning of Modern Austin* (Austin: University of Texas Press, 2010), 177–179.

11. Lobbyist quoted in *The Unforeseen*, a 2007 documentary on Barton Springs, directed by Laura Dunn.

12. Ken Solomon, "The Texas Lege's Culture War on Austin Has Come to a Cuddly Ceasefire," *Texas Monthly*, March 20, 2019, available at https://www.texasmonthly.com /politics/texas-legislature-cuddly-ceasefire/.

13. Ryan Robinson, quoted in Ken Martin, "Why Bother? Austin after 10–1," *Austin Bulldog*, April 29, 2013, available at http://www.theaustinbulldog.org/index.php?option= com_content&view=article&id=258:why-bother-austin-after-10-1&catid=3:main-articles.

14. Interviews with the author, July 5, 2018; July 11, 2018.

15. Richard Florida, *The Rise of the Creative Class: And How It's Transforming Work, Leisure, Community, and Everyday Life* (New York: Basic Books, 2002), 8.

16. Richard Florida, *Cities and the Creative Class* (New York: Routledge, 2005).

17. See, for example, Jamie Peck, "Struggling with the Creative Class," *International Journal of Urban and Regional Research* 29, no. 4 (December 2005): 740–770; Joel Kotkin, "Richard Florida Concedes the Limits of the Creative Class," *Daily Beast*, March 20, 2013, available at http://www.thedailybeast.com/articles/2013/03/20/richard-florida-concedes -the-limits-of-the-creative-class.html.

18. Richard Florida, *The Rise of the Creative Class—Revisited: 10th Anniversary Edition—Revised and Expanded* (New York: Basic Books, 2014).

19. The public opinion polling done by Peter Zandan underscores the prevalence of these sentiments among city residents. See Peter Zandan, "The Zandan Poll: Voices of the Austin Community: 2015 Poll Results," available at https://austinsurvey.files.wordpress .com/2015/03/zandan-poll-2015-voices-of-the-austin-community-c2ad-results.pdf; and "The Zandan Poll: Voices of the Austin Community: 2017 Poll Results," accessed March 19, 2018, available at https://austinsurvey.files.wordpress.com/2017/04/zandanpoll2017 _topline-final.pdf.

20. Richard Florida, "More Losers Than Winners in America's New Economic Geography," *CityLab*, January 30, 2013, http://www.citylab.com/work/2013/01/more-losers -winners-americas-new-economic-geography/4465/.

21. Javier Auyero, ed., "Introduction: Know Them Well," in *Invisible in Austin: Life and Labor in an American City* (Austin: University of Texas Press, 2015), 2.

22. Harvey Molotch, "The City as a Growth Machine: Toward a Political Economy of Place," *American Journal of Sociology* 82, no. 2 (September 1976): 309–332.

23. Eliot M. Tretter, *Shadows of a Sunbelt City: The Environment, Racism, and the Knowledge Economy in Austin* (Athens: University of Georgia Press, 2015), 134.

24. City of Austin, Environmental Commission, accessed October 4, 2017, available at https://austintexas.gov/envboard.

25. Swearingen, *Environmental City*, 189–193.

26. Swearingen, *Environmental City*, 173.

27. Michael A. Pagano and Ann O'M. Bowman, *Cityscapes and Capital: The Politics of Urban Development* (Baltimore, MD: Johns Hopkins University Press, 1995).

28. Interview with the author, June 7, 2017.

29. Michael Hall, "The City of the Eternal Boom," *Texas Monthly* (March 2016), 84–91, 151–161.

30. Jose Valera, as quoted in Hall, "City of the Eternal Boom," 160.

31. In 2017, the city launched a strategic planning process to inform its development of a coherent and viable vision for the future.

CHAPTER 1

1. David C. Humphrey, *Austin: A History of the Capital City* (Austin: Texas State Historical Association, 1997), 1.

2. Jeffrey Stuart Kerr, *Seat of Empire: The Embattled Birth of Austin, Texas* (Lubbock: Texas Tech University Press, 2013), chapter 6.

3. Legislation enacted in 2017 made it more difficult for cities with populations of five hundred thousand or more to annex adjacent land.

4. U.S. Census Bureau, American Fact Finder, "Annual Estimates of the Resident Population for Incorporated Places of 50,000 or More, Ranked by July 1, 2017 Population," American Fact Finder, May 2018, available at https://factfinder.census.gov/faces /tableservices/jsf/pages/productview.xhtml?src=bkmk.

5. Richard Florida, *The Rise of the Creative Class* (New York: Basic Books, 2002).

6. Joshua Long, as quoted in Kelli Ainsworth, Kelly Connelly, and Wells Dunbar, "What Draws People to Austin (And What Drives Them Away)," *KUT*, October 11, 2012, available at http://www.kut.org/post/what-draws-people-austin-and-what-drives-them -away.

7. Peter Zandan, "The Zandan Poll: Voices of the Austin Community: 2017 Poll Results," accessed February 1, 2018, available at https://austinsurvey.files.wordpress .com/2017/04/zandanpoll2017_topline-final.pdf.

8. City of Austin, Imagine Austin, accessed May 10, 2018, available at http://www .austintexas.gov/page/imagine-austin-vision.

9. Heinz Eulau and Kenneth Prewitt, *Labyrinths of Democracy: Adaptations, Linkages, Representation, and Policies in Urban Politics* (Indianapolis: Bobbs-Merrill, 1973), vii.

10. Eulau and Prewitt, *Labyrinths of Democracy*, 227.

11. Legislators who adjust their orientations to fit the issue are often referred to as "politicos."

12. Eulau and Prewitt, *Labyrinths of Democracy*, 218–225.

13. Dennis R. Judd and Todd Swanstrom, *City Politics: The Political Economy of Urban America* (New York: Pearson, 2006), chapter 4.

14. Judd and Swanstrom, *City Politics*, chapter 4.

15. Amy Bridges and Richard Kronick, "Writing the Rules to Win the Game: The Middle Class Regimes of Municipal Reformers," *Urban Affairs Review* 34, no. 5 (May 1999). Bridges and Kronick note also that reform success came more easily in places that had already enacted measures suppressing voter turnout. In Texas, legislation adopted in 1903 and 1905, which established a requirement that poll taxes be paid six months prior to the election, lowered the number of people registered to vote in many cities.

16. Peggy Heilig and Robert J. Mundt, *Your Voice at City Hall: The Politics, Procedures and Policies of District Representation* (Albany: State University of New York Press, 1984), 1.

17. Heilig and Mundt, *Your Voice at City Hall*, 1.

18. Hanna F. Pitkin, *The Concept of Representation* (Berkeley: University of California Press, 1967).

19. See the analysis of 139 cities and the related discussion in Albert K. Karnig, "Black Representation on City Councils: The Impact of District Elections and Socioeconomic Factors," *Urban Affairs Quarterly* 12, no. 2 (December 1976): 223–256.

20. Richard L. Engstrom and Michael D. McDonald, "The Election of Blacks to City Councils: Clarifying the Impact of Electoral Arrangements on the Seats/Population Relationship," *American Political Science Review* 75, no. 2 (June 1981): 344–354.

21. Susan A. MacManus, "City Council Election Procedures and Minority Representation: Are They Related?" *Social Science Quarterly* 59, no. 1 (June 1978): 153–161.

22. See, for example, the findings of Theodore P. Robinson and Thomas R. Dye, "Reformism and Black Representation on City Councils," *Social Science Quarterly* 59, no. 1 (June 1978): 133–141.

23. Engstrom and McDonald, "Election of Blacks to City Councils," 352.

24. Although some of the cities studied by Heilig and Mundt switched to districts for all council seats except the mayor, several of the cities operated with a mixed system that retained three or four at-large seats. These changes were the result of either local referenda on the question or pressure from the federal government.

25. Heilig and Mundt, *Your Voice at City Hall*, 85–86.

26. Heilig and Mundt, *Your Voice at City Hall*, 150.

27. J. L. Polinard, Robert D. Wrinkle, Tomas Longoria, and Norman E. Binder, *Electoral Structure and Urban Policy: The Impact on Mexican American Communities* (Armonk, NY: M. E. Sharpe, 1994).

28. Susan Welch and Timothy Bledsoe, *Urban Reform and Its Consequences: A Study in Representation* (Chicago: University of Chicago Press, 1988).

29. Welch and Bledsoe, *Urban Reform*, 77.

30. Welch and Bledsoe, *Urban Reform*, 100.

31. Welch and Bledsoe, *Urban Reform*, 110. For whites, the impact of education was much more important in influencing feelings of political efficacy. More educated whites felt more efficacious regardless of the electoral system.

32. James H. Svara, *Two Decades of Continuity and Change in American City Councils*, (Washington, DC: National League of Cities, 2003), 13.

33. Zoltan Hajnal and Jessica Trounstine, "Where Turnout Matters: The Consequences of Uneven Turnout in City Politics," *Journal of Politics* 67, no. 2 (May 2005): 515–535.

34. Hajnal and Trounstine, "Where Turnout Matters," 526.

35. Jessica Trounstine and Melody E. Valdini, "The Context Matters: The Effects of Single-Member versus At-Large Districts on City Council Diversity," *American Journal of Political Science*, 52, no. 3 (July 2008): 554–569.

36. Alistair Clark and Timothy B. Krebs, "Elections and Policy Responsiveness," in *Oxford Handbook of Urban Politics*, ed. Karen Mossberger, Susan E. Clarke, and Peter John (New York: Oxford University Press, 2012), 87–113.

37. Eulau and Prewitt, *Labyrinths of Democracy*, 613.

38. Bob Rescorla, Molly Hults, and Rusty Heckaman, "Brief Overview of the City of Austin's Government Structure Establishment and Evolution," in *City of Austin Resource Guide* (Austin: Austin History Center, 2017), 4.

39. Rescorla, Hults, and Heckaman, "Brief Overview of Austin's Government Structure."

40. Frank Staniszewski, "Ideology and Practice in Municipal Government Reform: A Case Study of Austin," *Studies in Politics*, series 1, paper no. 8 (Austin: University of Texas, 1977), 20–21.

41. David M. Olson, *Nonpartisan Elections: A Case Analysis* (Austin: University of Texas Press, 1965), 7–8.

42. Zilker had purchased a 350-acre tract of land in 1906 that included Barton Springs and later gave the tract to the local school board, which sold it to the city. Zilker, who had commented that "Austin can be made the most beautiful city in America," won the Austin's Most Worthy Citizen Award in 1928. Over time, the city installed numerous infrastructure improvements and developed the land to become Zilker Park, which, along with Barton Springs, is considered to be one of Austin's distinctive resources. See the discussion in Andrew M. Busch, *City in a Garden: Environmental Transformations and Racial Justice in Twentieth-Century Austin, Texas* (Chapel Hill: University of North Carolina Press, 2017), 72–73, 214–215.

43. Amy Bridges, *Morning Glories: Municipal Reform in the Southwest* (Princeton, NJ: Princeton University Press, 1997), 91.

44. Staniszewski, "Ideology and Practice in Municipal Government Reform," 21.

45. Staniszewski, "Ideology and Practice in Municipal Government Reform," 23.

46. A commission structure was created in Galveston in the aftermath of a devastating hurricane in which approximately six thousand to eight thousand people died and most of the structures in the city were reduced to rubble. The apparent inability of the incumbent city council to design and implement a rebuilding plan led the wealthy, influential businessmen to devise an alternative governmental structure: a five-member governing board called a commission. To these business leaders turned reformers, a commission would achieve an objective they had long favored: the replacement of politics with more efficient, businesslike principles. Their plan was approved by the state legislature, with three commissioners appointed by the governor and two elected at large by Galveston voters. Facing legal challenges that the appointment of commissioners was unconstitutional, the plan was eventually modified to provide for the election of all five commissioners. See the discussion in Bradley Robert Rice, *Progressive Cities: The Commission Government Movement in America, 1901–1920* (Austin: University of Texas Press, 1977), chapter 1.

47. Bradley Robert Rice, "Commission Form of City Government," Texas State Historical Association, accessed May 19, 2018, available at https://tshaonline.org/handbook/online/articles/moc01.

48. Staniszewski, "Ideology and Practice in Municipal Government Reform," 25–27.

49. Rescorla, Hults, and Heckaman, "Brief Overview of Austin's Government Structure."

50. Stuart A. MacCorkle, *Austin's Three Forms of Government* (San Antonio: Naylor, 1973), 63.

51. Staniszewski, "Ideology and Practice in Municipal Government Reform," 29.

52. In 1913, Amarillo had become the first city in Texas to adopt a council-manager form of government. See Terrell Blodgett, "Council-Manager Form of City Government," Texas State Historical Association, accessed January 5, 2018, available at https://tshaonline.org/handbook/online/articles/moc02.

53. Harold A. Stone, Don K. Price, and Kathryn H. Stone. *City Manager Government in Nine Cities* (Chicago: Public Administration Service, 1940), 428.

54. Stone, Price, and Stone, *City Manager Government in Nine Cities*, 429.

55. Tom Miller would go on to serve twenty-three years as mayor of Austin.

56. Bridges, *Morning Glories*, 98.

57. Trounstine contends that business-oriented reformers functioned as a political monopoly in Austin from the early 1950s to the early 1970s, enjoying electoral success and policy dominance. See Jessica Trounstine, *Political Monopolies in American Cities: The Rise and Fall of Bosses and Reformers* (Chicago: University of Chicago Press, 2008).

58. Richard L. Engstrom and Richard N. Engstrom, "The Majority Vote Rule and Runoff Primaries in the United States," *Electoral Studies* 27, no. 3 (September 2008): 407–416.

59. Trounstine, *Political Monopolies in American Cities*, 31.

60. Anthony Orum, *Power, Money and the People: The Making of Modern Austin* (Austin: Texas Monthly Press, 1987), 219.

61. Orum, *Power, Money and the People*, 222.

62. A black candidate for city council, Arthur DeWitty, had finished eighth out of fourteen candidates in the 1951 election. See the discussion in Staniszewski, "Ideology and Practice in Municipal Government Reform," 42.

63. Staniszewski, "Ideology and Practice in Municipal Government Reform," 44.

64. Place 7 became the mayor's seat.

65. Orum, *Power, Money and the People*, 295–298.

66. Staniszewski, "Ideology and Practice in Municipal Government Reform," 45.

67. William Scott Swearingen Jr. *Environmental City: People, Place, Politics and the Meaning of Modern Austin* (Austin: University of Texas Press 2010), 127–133.

68. Swearingen, *Environmental City*, 189–193.

69. Eliot M. Tretter, *Shadows of a Sunbelt City: The Environment, Racism, and the Knowledge Economy in Austin* (Athens: University of Georgia Press, 2015), chapter 5.

70. Busch, *City in a Garden*, 240–247.

71. City of Austin, Office of the City Manager, accessed May 27, 2018, available at https://www.austintexas.gov/department/city-manager.

CHAPTER 2

1. Office of the City Clerk, Election History, accessed June 1, 2018, available at http://www.ci.austin.tx.us/election/byrecord.cfm?eid=143.

2. Austin Charter Revision Committee Records, AR.2006.004 (Austin: Austin History Center, 2006).

3. Houston and Dallas retained some at-large seats on its council; however, the majority of the council was to be elected from geographically designated districts. In 1990, Dallas expanded its council and made all of the seats, except the mayor's, district based. Houston has retained its hybrid system.

4. Robert Brischetto, Charles L. Cotrell, and R. Michael Stevens, "Conflict and Change in the Political Culture of San Antonio in the 1970s," in *The Politics of San Antonio: Community, Progress, and Power*, ed. David R. Johnson, John A. Booth, and Richard J. Harris (Lincoln: University of Nebraska Press, 1983), 87–88.

5. Amy Bridges, *Morning Glories: Municipal Reform in the Southwest* (Princeton, NJ: Princeton University Press, 1997), 190–191.

6. J. L. Polinard, Robert D. Wrinkle, Tomas Longoria, and Norman E. Binder, *Electoral Structure and Urban Policy: The Impact of Mexican American Communities* (Armonk, NY: M. E. Sharpe, 1994), 25–26.

7. Sarah Coppola, "Austin Voters Rejected City Council Districts Six Times in the Past. Will This Year Be Different?" *Austin American-Statesman*, September 15, 2012, available at https://www.statesman.com/news/local/austin-voters-rejected-city-council-districts-six-times-the-past-will-this-year-different/koR4lTOGOpzbeRKrBbCCPM/.

8. See the comments of Ed Wendler Sr. in Coppola, "Austin Voters Rejected."

9. Wells Dunbar, "David Van Os on Single-Member Districts," *Austin Chronicle*, February 28, 2008, available at http://www.austinchronicle.com/daily/news/2008-02-28/597508.

10. Ed Wendler Sr., as quoted in Coppola, "Austin Voters Rejected."

11. Office of the City Clerk, Election History, April 1, 1978, available at http://www.ci.austin.tx.us/election/byrecord.cfm?eid=133.

12. Coppola, "Austin Voters Rejected."

13. *Volma Overton et al., v. City of Austin*, 871 F.2d 529 (1989).

14. City of Austin, Office of the City Clerk, Election History, May 7, 1988, available at http://www.ci.austin.tx.us/election/byrecord.cfm?eid=133.

15. Eliot M. Tretter, *Shadows of a Sunbelt City: The Environment, Racism, and the Knowledge Economy in Austin* (Athens: University of Georgia Press, 2015).

16. City of Austin, Office of the City Clerk, Election History, May 7, 1994, available at http://www.ci.austin.tx.us/election/byrecord.cfm?eid=133.

17. The council delayed placing a citizens' initiative on the ballot to save Barton Springs from development and pollution, and, when it eventually did schedule balloting, the council included an alternative ordinance designed to undercut the citizens' initiative.

18. "A Way to Better Representation," *Austin American-Statesman*, January 22, 2000, A14.

19. One of the CRC's recommendations was to adopt instant runoff voting in which voters rank candidates in individual races to avoid the need for a runoff if no one receives a majority of the votes. This recommendation did not appear on the ballot.

20. "Council's Attempt at New Voting Districts Misses the Point," *Austin American-Statesman*, April 8, 2002, A14.

21. Coppola, "Austin Voters Rejected."

22. Coppola, "Austin Voters Rejected."

23. David Van Os, as quoted in Dunbar, "David Van Os."

24. Interview with the author, July 11, 2018.

25. Ken Martin, "Maps Prove a Select Few Govern Austin: Forty Years of Election History Expose Extent of Disparities," *Austin Bulldog*, August 2011, available at https://www.theaustinbulldog.org/index.php?option=com_content&view=article&id=150:at-large-elections-favor-anglo-choices&catid=3:main-articles#comment-213.

26. Wells Dunbar, "The Single-Member Situation: Movement Afoot—Once Again—to Ask Voters to Approve City Council Districts," *Austin Chronicle*, February 25, 2011, available at https://www.austinchronicle.com/news/2011-02-25/the-single-member-situation/.

27. Josh Rosenblatt, "Citizens Group Sees African-American Plurality in 10–1 Districting Plan," *Austin Monitor*, July 9, 2012, available at https://www.austinmonitor.com/stories/2012/07/citizens-group-sees-african-american-plurality-in-10-1-districting-plan/.

28. Interview with the author, July 5, 2018.

29. Lee Leffingwell, as quoted in Josh Rosenblatt, "Geopolitical Fault Lines: Austin's Latest Attempt at Single-Member Districts Is Getting a Mixed Response," *Austin Chronicle*, July 6, 2012, available at https://www.austinchronicle.com/news/2012-07-06/Geopolitical-Fault-Lines/.

30. Rosenblatt, "Geopolitical Fault Lines."

31. Sarah Coppola, "City Offers Residents 2 District Scenarios," *Austin American-Statesman*, June 30, 2012, A1, A11.

32. Sarah Coppola, "Pros and Cons of Council Districts," *Austin American-Statesman*, September 24, 2012, A1, A4.

33. Ken Martin, "8–2–1 Plan Near-Certain to Go on Ballot," *Austin Bulldog*, July 31, 2012, available at https://www.theaustinbulldog.org/index.php?option=com_content&view=article&id=208:8-2-1-plan-certain-to-go-on-ballot&catid=3:main-articles.

34. The proposition authorized each member of the city council to strike one applicant from the pool, if desired. No council members invoked this option.

35. City of Austin, Ordinance No. 20120802-015, August 2, 2012, available at http://www.austintexas.gov/edims/document.cfm?id=174695.

36. Sarah Coppola, "Observers: Door-to-Door Effort Fueled Prop. 3 Win," *Austin American-Statesman*, November 8, 2012, B1, B7.

37. Josh Rosenblatt, "Geopolitical Fault Lines."

38. The environmental community appeared to have been split on whether there was any advantage to their interests with the retention of some at-large seats on the council. More than one interviewee indicated that environmentalists and developers often reach an accommodation such that each can achieve some of its objectives when it comes to specific projects.

39. Interview with the author, July 5, 2018.

40. Interview with the author, July 11, 2018.

41. Richard Florida, *Cities and the Creative Class* (New York: Routledge, 2005); see also Carl Grodach, "Before and after the Creative City: The Politics of Urban Cultural Policy in Austin, Texas," *Journal of Urban Affairs* 34, no. 1 (2012): 81–97.

42. Joshua Long, *Weird City: Sense of Place and Creative Resistance in Austin, Texas* (Austin: University of Texas Press, 2010).

43. Bobby Blanchard, "Austin City Council Primed for an Ideological Shift in November," *New York Times*, October 7, 2014, available at https://www.nytimes.com/2014/10/03/us/austin-city-council-is-primed-for-an-ideological-shift-in-november.html?_r=0.

44. Interview with the author, July 11, 2018.

45. Some large cities such as Houston, Philadelphia, Jacksonville, and Indianapolis continue to elect some council members at large, but the majority of their councils are elected from districts. When Seattle replaced its at-large system in 2013, it created seven district seats and retained two at-large seats. As of 2019, Columbus, Ohio, was the largest city to elect its entire council at-large.

46. Interview with the author, May 2, 2019.

47. Tretter, *Shadows of a Sunbelt City*, 119, 139.

48. City of Austin, Proposition 3 Results: The 10–1 Plan, November 6, 2012, available at http://www.austintexas.gov/sites/default/files/files/Planning/Demographics/Prop_3_2012.pdf.

49. Joshua G. Behr, *Race, Ethnicity, and the Politics of City Redistricting: Minority-Opportunity Districts and the Election of Hispanics and Blacks to City Councils* (Albany: State University of New York Press, 2004), 112.

50. Behr, *Race, Ethnicity*, 104.

51. *Shelby County v. Holder*, 570 U.S. 2 (2013).

52. Independent Citizens Redistricting Commission, Final Report, City of Austin, October 24, 2014, available at http://www.austintexas.gov/edims/document.cfm?id=222387.

53. Independent Citizens Redistricting Commission, Final Report.

54. Elizabeth Pagano, "The More (Maps) the Merrier! A Brief Introduction to the ICRC's Proposed City Council District Map—and a Few Alternatives," *Austin Chronicle*, October 25, 2013, available at https://www.austinchronicle.com/news/2013-10-25/the-more-maps-the-merrier/.

55. City of Austin, District Demographics and Maps, accessed March 25, 2018, available at http://www.austintexas.gov//page/district-demographics.

CHAPTER 3

1. The mayor's term of office was set at four years.

2. Zoltan L. Hajnal, *America's Uneven Democracy: Race, Turnout, and Representation in City Politics* (New York: Cambridge University Press, 2010), 166.

3. City of Austin, Office of the City Clerk, Election History, accessed April 24, 2018, available at http://www.ci.austin.tx.us/election/byrecord.cfm?eid=30.

4. District 6 includes a small portion of Austin that, due to annexations, spills into Williamson County. An argument can be made that residents of that area may be less interested in Austin politics. See the data and discussion in Stefan Haag, "Voter Turnout and Representation in the Austin City Council Elections, 2014" (Austin: Austin Community College Center for Public Policy and Political Studies, November 2015), 1.

5. Three council candidates had received a majority of the votes cast in their districts, thereby avoiding a runoff.

6. Hajnal, *America's Uneven Democracy*, 140.

7. The effect is especially pronounced when groups are organized and voter turnout is low. See the research reported in Sarah F. Anzia, *Timing and Turnout: How Off-Cycle Elections Favor Organized Groups* (Chicago: University of Chicago Press, 2014).

8. Chris Tausanovitch and Christopher Warshaw, "Representation in Municipal Government," *American Political Science Review*, 108, no. 3 (August 2014), 605.

9. Peggy Heilig and Robert J. Mundt, *Your Voice at City Hall: The Politics, Procedures and Policies of District Representation* (Albany: State University of New York Press, 1984), 17, 70–76.

10. Heilig and Mundt, *Your Voice at City Hall*, 76.

11. Susan Welch and Timothy Bledsoe, *Urban Reform and Its Consequences: A Study in Representation* (Chicago: University of Chicago Press, 1988), 112.

12. See, for example, the discussions in Anthony Gierzynski and David Breaux, "Money and Votes in State Legislative Elections," *Legislative Studies Quarterly* 16, no. 2 (May 1991): 203–217; Gary C. Jacobson, "The Effects of Campaign Spending in Congressional Elections," *American Political Science Review* 72, no. 2 (June 1978): 469–491; Randall W. Partin, "Assessing the Impact of Campaign Spending in Governors' Races," *Political Research Quarterly* 55, no. 1 (March 2002): 213–233; Nicholas R. Seabrook, "Money and State Legislative Elections: The Conditional Impact of Political Context," *American Politics Research* 38, no. 3 (May 2010): 399–424; Timothy B. Krebs, "Political Experience and Fundraising in City Council Elections," *Social Science Quarterly* 82, no. 3 (September 2001): 536–551.

13. Ken Martin, "10–1 Elections Cost $6.3 Million: Political Action Committees Laid Out $726,000 for Independent Expenditures to Influence Voters," *Austin Bulldog*, March 27, 2015, available at https://www.theaustinbulldog.org/index.php?option=com_content&view=article&id=342:10-1-elections-cost-63-million&catid=3:main-articles.

14. Lilly Rockwell, "What Will New Republican Members Bring to Austin City Council?" *Austin American-Statesman*, December 17, 2014, available at https://www.mystatesman.com/news/what-will-new-republican-members-bring-austin-city-council/Q3Su8Z7eudklhYzDp7HvEK/.

15. See the discussion in Jessica Trounstine and Melody E. Valdini, "The Context Matters: The Effects of Single-Member versus At-Large Districts on City Council Diversity," *American Journal of Political Science* 52, no. 3 (July 2008): 555.

16. Mirya R. Holman, *Women in Politics in the American City* (Philadelphia: Temple University Press, 2015), 23.

17. Lilly Rockwell, "As Women Take Majority on Austin City Council, Staff Warned to Expect More Questions, Longer Talks," *Austin American-Statesman*, May 15, 2015, available at http://cityhall.blog.statesman.com/2015/05/12/as-women-take-majority-on-austin-city-council-staff-warned-to-expect-more-questions-longer-talks/.

18. Lilly Rockwell, "Austin Council Members Fuming about City-Led Training Session on Women," *Austin American-Statesman*, May 13, 2015, available at https://www.mystatesman.com/news/local/austin-council-members-fuming-about-city-led-training-session-women/fIURkxmCimnsSAY1GEj5DN/.

19. Heilig and Mundt, *Your Voice at City Hall*, 70.

20. Welch and Bledsoe, *Urban Reform*, 46.

21. This is similar to the classification scheme developed by Carnes. See Nicholas Carnes, "Does the Numerical Underrepresentation of the Working Class in Congress Matter?" *Legislative Studies Quarterly* 37, no. 1 (February 2012): 5–34.

22. This finding comports with research that analyzed the occupational status of nearly three thousand mayoral candidates in more than two hundred U.S. cities over fifty years. Only 4 percent of mayoral candidates were employed in occupations that were considered working-class occupations. See Patricia A. Kirkland, "Social Class and Representation in American Cities," working paper, August 25, 2018.

23. Ken Martin, "An Economically Diverse City Council: City No Longer Governed Only by Very Well-to-Do Citizens," *Austin Bulldog*, June 15, 2015, available at https://www.theaustinbulldog.org/index.php?option=com_content&view=article&id=354%3Aan-economically-diverse-city-council&catid=3%3Amain-articles&Itemid=15.

24. Heinz Eulau and Kenneth Prewitt, *Labyrinths of Democracy: Adaptations, Linkages, Representation, and Policies in Urban Politics* (Indianapolis: Bobbs-Merrill, 1973), chapter 28.

25. Welch and Bledsoe, *Urban Reform*, 94; Jessica Trounstine, "Representation and Accountability in Cities," *Annual Review of Political Science*, 13 (2010): 409.

26. Heilig and Mundt, *Your Voice at City Hall*, 20.

27. Welch and Bledsoe, *Urban Reform*, 97.

28. Heilig and Mundt, *Your Voice at City Hall*, 20.

29. Interviews with the author, June 26, 2018; August 16, 2018.

30. Craig M. Burnett and Vladimir Kogan, "Local Logrolling: Assessing the Impact of Legislative Districts in Los Angeles," *Urban Affairs Review* 50, no. 5 (September 2014): 648–671.

31. Edward C. Banfield and James Q. Wilson, *City Politics* (Cambridge, MA: Harvard University Press, 1963).

32. Burnett and Kogan, "Local Logrolling."

33. VoteTracker, *Austin American-Statesman*, accessed April 9–20, 2018, available at https://apps.statesman.com/votetracker/entities/austin-city-council/.

34. Heilig and Mundt, *Your Voice at City Hall,* 147.

35. Heilig and Mundt, *Your Voice at City Hall*, 151.

36. Kaufmann's study of mayoral elections showed that local elections generally revolve around allocatable issues, particularly the distribution of services. See Karen M. Kaufmann, *The Urban Voter: Group Conflict and Mayoral Voting Behavior in American Cities* (Ann Arbor: University of Michigan Press, 2004).

37. The selected topics are reflective of similar subjects tracked by the *Austin American-Statesman*'s VoteTracker, a project that collects information on city council voting. Available at https://apps.statesman.com/votetracker/.

38. The prevalence of development as an agenda item in city councils is common. See the findings of Holman, *Women in Politics in the American City*, chapter 3.

39. Nick Barbaro, "Public Notice: First, Do No Harm," *Austin Chronicle*, February 6, 2015, available at https://www.austinchronicle.com/news/2015-02-06/public-notice-first-do-no-harm/.

40. Elizabeth Pagano, "New Council Plans to Change Meetings, Committees," *KUT*, January 9, 2015, available at http://www.kut.org/post/new-council-plans-change-meetings-committees.

41. City of Austin, Ordinance No. 20150129-026, January 29, 2015, available at http://www.austintexas.gov/edims/document.cfm?id=225685.

42. Christopher Neely, "Austin City Council Officially Slashes Its Committee Structure," *Community Impact*, February 16, 2017, available at https://communityimpact.com/austin/city-county/2017/02/16/austin-city-council-officially-slashes-committee-structure/.

43. Interview with the author, August 16, 2018.

44. Susan Nold and Christopher Kennedy, "It's Up to the People of Austin to Make Meaningful Change Out of the '10–1' System," *UT News*, November 17, 2015, available at https://news.utexas.edu/2015/11/17/making-meaningful-change-out-of-the-10-1-system.

45. Heilig and Mundt, *Your Voice at City Hall*, chapter 5.

46. Interview with the author, August 16, 2018.

47. Lilly Rockwell, "What Do Austin Residents Think of the City Council," *Austin American-Statesman*, January 16, 2016, available at http://cityhall.blog.statesman.com/2016/01/15/what-do-austin-residents-think-of-the-city-council/.

48. Nolan Hicks, "Austin City Manager Marc Ott Leaving for Washington Job," *Austin American-Statesman*, August 12, 2016, available at https://www.mystatesman

.com/news/local/austin-city-manager-marc-ott-leaving-for-washington-job/9TY6MG
22oRQIiCECiNY9cI/.

49. Nolan Hicks, "Austin City Manager."

50. Nolan Hicks, "Austin Council Gives City Manager Marc Ott a $22,000 Raise,"
Austin American-Statesman, June 14, 2016, available at https://www.mystatesman.com
/news/local-govt--politics/austin-council-gives-city-manager-marc-ott-000-raise/CMi
FRV4CJXLvGC9JImG1RK/.

51. Interview with the author, July 5, 2018.

52. Interview with the author, June 26, 2018.

53. Alison Alter, as quoted in Calily Bien, "Austin Names Spencer Cronk as New
City Manager," KXAN, December 19, 2017, available at https://www.kxan.com/news
/local/austin/austin-names-spencer-cronk-as-new-city-manager/1031446409.

54. Elizabeth Findell, "Austin City Manager Will Replace Executive Team after
Open Recruitment," *Austin American-Statesman*, July 27, 2018, available at https://
www.statesman.com/news/local/austin-city-manager-will-replace-executive-team-after
-open-recruitment/k4vm8xqD9hiGq5N3w2axHN/.

55. Spencer Cronk, as quoted in Michael King, "Cronk to Reorganize Management
Team," *Austin Chronicle*, August 3, 2018, available at https://www.austinchronicle.com
/news/2018-08-03/cronk-to-reorganize-management-team/.

56. Interview with the author, July 5, 2018.

57. City of Austin, "Memorandum: Assessment of Fiscal Impact for Charter Amendments," August 29, 2012, 1–2.

58. Lilly Rockwell, "Austin City Council Staffing Plan Grows, but Not as Mayor
Had Hoped," *Austin American-Statesman*, March 31, 2015, available at https://www
.mystatesman.com/news/local/austin-city-council-staffing-plan-grows-but-not-mayor
-had-hoped/UGXKvnz8FsoBmCx9IOnu7J/.

59. Lilly Rockwell, "Austin City Council and Mayor Approve Plan for More Staff,"
Austin American-Statesman, September 24, 2016, available at https://statesman.com/NEWS
/20160924/Austin-City-Council-and-mayor-approve-plan-for-more-staff.

60. Peter Zandan, "The Zandan Poll: Voices of the Austin Community: 2015 Poll
Results," accessed February 1, 2018, available at https://austinsurvey.files.wordpress
.com/2015/03/zandan-poll-2015-voices-of-the-austin-community-c2ad-results.pdf.

61. Peter Zandan, "The Zandan Poll: Voices of the Austin Community: 2017 Poll
Results," accessed February 1, 2018, available at https://austinsurvey.files.wordpress
.com/2017/04/zandanpoll2017_topline-final.pdf.

62. Andra Lim, "How Did Each Austin City Council Member Perform in 2015,"
Austin American-Statesman, January 15, 2016, available at https://www.statesman.com
/news/20160904/how-did-each-austin-city-council-member-perform-in-2015.

63. City of Austin, "Survey Shows Satisfaction with City Services Rising," February
21, 2019, available at http://wwwaustintexas.gov/news/survey-shows-satisfaction-city
-services-rising.

64. Nolan Hicks and Elizabeth Findell, "What Will Addition of Alter, Flannigan
Bring to Austin City Council?" *Austin American-Statesman*, January 15, 2016, available at
https://www.mystatesman.com/news/local/how-did-each-austin-city-council-member
-perform-2015/cjRONuhnZQOzm2s9WdcwKN/.

65. Hajnal, *America's Uneven Democracy*, 166.

66. Stefan Haag, Jeff Smith, and William R. "Peck" Young, "Studies of Political Statistics: Voter Turnout in Two Austin City Council Districts: 2014 and 2016" (Austin: Austin Community College Center for Public Policy and Political Studies, March 2017).

67. Elizabeth Findell, "Jimmy Flannigan, Alison Alter Bring Sophomore Shift to City Council," *Austin American-Statesman*, June 11, 2018, available at https://www.mystatesman.com/news/local-govt--politics/jimmy-flannigan-alison-alter-bring-sophomore-shift-city-council/Sx5VnG2riEQsPVtX9R3ohI/.

68. Travis County Clerk, City of Austin Election Results, accessed May 8, 2019, available at http://traviselectionresults.com/enr/results/display.do;jsessionid=96ecb67cc9c79f688c96c537a7d0?criteria.electionId=20181106&formSubmitted=1.

69. Will Anderson, "Austin Election Results: Next City Council to Feature More Urbanists but No Conservatives," *Austin Business Journal*, December 12, 2018, available at https://www.bizjournals.com/austin/news/2018/12/12/austin-election-results-next-citycouncil-to.html.

70. Philip Jankowski, "For Good or Bad, Petition Elections a Growing Trend in Texas," *Austin American-Statesman*, January 24, 2019, available at https://www.statesman.com/news/20190124/for-good-or-bad-petition-elections-growing-trend-in-texas.

71. Steve Adler, accessed May 8, 2019, available at www.austintexas.gov/department/mayor.

72. Delia Garza, as quoted in Nina Hernandez, "Rebooted City Council Gets a New Chance to Fix Austin," *Austin Chronicle*, January 11, 2019, available at https://www.austinchronicle.com/news/2019-01-11/rebooted-city-council-gets-a-new-chance-to-fix-austin/.

73. U.S. News and World Report, "125 Best Places to Live in the USA," accessed April 8, 2019, available at https://realestate.usnews.com/places/rankings/best-places-to-live.

CONCLUSION

1. See, for example, some of the earliest empirical work, such as Albert K. Karnig, "Black Representation on City Councils: The Impact of District Elections and Socioeconomic Factors," *Urban Affairs Quarterly* 12, no. 2 (December 1976): 223–256; Richard L. Engstrom and Michael D. McDonald, "The Election of Blacks to City Councils: Clarifying the Impact of Electoral Arrangements on the Seats/Population Relationship," *American Political Science Review* 75, no. 2 (June 1981): 344–354; Peggy Heilig and Robert J. Mundt, *Your Voice at City Hall: The Politics, Procedures and Policies of District Representation* (Albany: State University of New York Press, 1984); Susan Welch and Timothy Bledsoe, *Urban Reform and Its Consequences: A Study in Representation* (Chicago: University of Chicago Press, 1988); J. L. Polinard, Robert D. Wrinkle, Tomas Longoria, and Norman E. Binder, *Electoral Structure and Urban Policy: The Impact on Mexican American Communities* (Armonk, NY: M. E. Sharpe, 1994).

2. Recent research on the Los Angeles City Council provides some limited reassurance that moving from an at-large electoral system to a district-based system does not necessarily usher in rampant parochialism and logrolling in the council. See Craig M. Burnett and Vladimir Kogan, "Local Logrolling? Assessing the Impact of Legislative Districting in Los Angeles," *Urban Affairs Review* 50, no. 5 (September 2014): 648–671.

3. Michael King, "Point Austin: Strange Bedfellows, Stranger Politics," *Austin Chronicle*, August 10, 2018, available at https://www.austinchronicle.com/news/2018-08-10/point-austin-strange-bedfellows-stranger-politics/.

4. Philip Jankowski, "Petition Filed to Require an Efficiency Audit of Austin City Hall," *Austin American-Statesman*, July 13, 2018, available at https://www.statesman.com/news/local/petition-filed-require-efficiency-audit-austin-cityhall/t7CqUKaXqWF3UDgo7vblnM/.

5. Philip Jankowski, "Did Backers of City Audit Proposition Skirt 'Dark Money' Restrictions," *Austin American-Statesman*, September 25, 2018, available at https://www.statesman.com/news/20180918/did-backers-of-city-audit-proposition-skirt-dark-money-restrictions.

6. Ken Martin, "Council's Ballot Language Triggers Lawsuit(s)," *Austin Bulldog*, August 11, 2018, available at https://www.theaustinbulldog.org/index.php?option=com_content&view=article&id=430:councils-ballot-language-triggers-lawsuits&catid=3:main-articles.

7. Michael King, "Point Austin: What You Say, and How You Say It," *Austin Chronicle*, August 17, 2018, available at https://www.austinchronicle.com/news/2018-08-17/point-austin-what-you-say-and-how-you-say-it/.

8. City of Austin, Office of the City Clerk, Election History, November 6, 2018, available at http://www.austintexas.gov/election/byrecord.cfm?eid=205.

9. Syeda Hasan, "Council Votes Unanimously to Scrap CodeNEXT," *Austin Monitor*, August 10, 2018, available at https://www.austinmonitor.com/stories/2018/08/city-council-votes-unanimously-to-scrap-codenext/.

10. Nick Barbaro, "Public Notice: The Battle Is Joined," *Austin Chronicle*, August 24, 2018, available at https://www.austinchronicle.com/news/2018-08-24/public-notice-the-battle-is-joined/.

11. Bridget Grumet, "Poll Shows How We're Split over CodeNext and What Issue Can Bring Us Together," *Austin American-Statesman*, May 11, 2018, available at http://viewpoints.blog.mystatesman.com/2018/05/11/poll-shows-how-were-split-over-codenext-and-what-issue-can-bring-us-together/.

12. Richard Florida, *The New Urban Crisis* (New York: Basic Books, 2017). Florida is referring to metropolitan areas, which in Austin's case includes Travis County and four surrounding counties. The problems identified in *The New Urban Crisis* spill beyond Austin's borders, but they are of central concern within the city's limits.

13. Lawsuits were filed against the city, and, as a result, Austin's ordinance was put on hold by a state appeals court while it reviewed the legal case.

14. Jaweed Kaleem, "'Freedom City'? Going beyond 'Sanctuary,' Austin, Texas, Vows to Curtail Arrests," *Los Angeles Times*, June 19, 2018, available at http://www.latimes.com/nation/la-na-austin-freedom-city-2018-story.html.

15. Mark Lisheron, "Austin City Council Goes Heavy on Affordable Housing in a Major Bond Issue," *Texas Monitor*, July 2, 2018, available at https://texasmonitor.org/austin-city-concil-goes-heavy-on-affordable-housing-in-a-major-bond-issue/.

16. Bruce Katz, "Envisioning the New Localism," *Public Management* 100, no. 1 (January–February 2018): 6–9.

17. Robert Reinhold, "Booming Austin Fears It Will Lose Its Charms," *New York Times*, October 8, 1983, available at https://www.nytimes.com/1983/10/08/us/booming-austin-fears-it-will-lose-its-charms.html.

18. Emblematic of this concern is Austinites' ambivalent reaction to the chamber's bid to attract Amazon's second headquarters. The reluctance involved the likelihood of increased traffic problems, higher costs of living, and a threat to the city's "quirky culture." Sebastian Herrera, "A Year into Amazon's Much-Hyped HQ2 Search, Austin—and the Other Finalists—Are Still Waiting," *512Tech by Austin American-Statesman*, September 4, 2018, available at https://www.512tech.com/technology/year-into-amazon-much-hyped-hq2-search-austin-and-the-other-finalists-are-still-waiting/iMLYo8igcVQEEHb3S7TlRJ/?utm_source=newspaper&utm_medium=email&utm_campaign=5736906&ecmp=newspaper_email&.

BIBLIOGRAPHY

Ancia, Sarah F. *Timing and Turnout: How Off-Cycle Elections Favor Organized Groups.* Chicago: University of Chicago Press, 2014.

Anderson, Will. "Austin Election Results: Next City Council to Feature More Urbanists but No Conservatives." *Austin Business Journal*, December 12, 2018.

Austin History Center. *Austin Charter Revision Committee Records* (AR.2006.004). 2006.

Auyero, Javier. "Introduction: Know Them Well." In *Invisible in Austin: Life and Labor in an American City*, edited by Javier Auyero. Austin: University of Texas Press, 2015.

Banfield, Edward C., and James Q. Wilson. *City Politics.* Cambridge, MA: Harvard University Press, 1963.

Barbaro, Nick. "Public Notice: The Battle Is Joined." *Austin Chronicle*, August 24, 2018. Available at https://www.austinchronicle.com/news/2018-08-24/public-notice-the -battle-is-joined/.

———. "Public Notice: First, Do No Harm." *Austin Chronicle*, February 6, 2015. Available at https://www.austinchronicle.com/news/2015-02-06/public-notice-first-do -no-harm/.

Behr, Joshua G. *Race, Ethnicity, and the Politics of City Redistricting: Minority-Opportunity Districts and the Election of Hispanics and Blacks to City Councils.* Albany: State University of New York Press, 2004.

Bien, Calily. "Austin Names Spencer Cronk as New City Manager." KXAN, December 19, 2017.

Blanchard, Bobby. "Austin City Council Primed for an Ideological Shift in November." *New York Times*, October 7, 2014. Available at https://www.nytimes.com/2014/10/03 /us/austin-city-council-is-primed-for-an-ideological-shift-in-november.html?_r=0.

Blodgett, Terrell. "Council-Manager Form of City Government." Austin: Texas State Historical Association. Accessed January 5, 2018. Available at https://tshaonline .org/handbook/online/articles/moc02.

Bridges, Amy. *Morning Glories: Municipal Reform in the Southwest.* Princeton, NJ: Princeton University Press, 1997.

Bridges, Amy, and Richard Kronick. "Writing the Rules to Win the Game: The Middle-Class Regimes of Municipal Reformers." *Urban Affairs Review* 34, no. 5 (1999): 691–706.

Brischetto, Robert, Charles L. Cotrell, and R. Michael Stevens. "Conflict and Change in the Political Culture of San Antonio in the 1970s." In *The Politics of San Antonio: Community, Progress, and Power,* edited by David R. Johnson, John A. Booth, and Richard J. Harris. Lincoln: University of Nebraska Press, 1983.

Burnett, Craig M., and Vladimir Kogan. "Local Logrolling? Assessing the Impact of Legislative Districting in Los Angeles." *Urban Affairs Review* 50, no. 5 (2014): 648–671.

Busch, Andrew M. *City in a Garden: Environmental Transformations and Racial Justice in Twentieth-Century Austin, Texas.* Chapel Hill: University of North Carolina Press, 2017.

Carnes, Nicholas. "Does the Numerical Underrepresentation of the Working Class in Congress Matter?" *Legislative Studies Quarterly* 37, no. 1 (2012): 5–34.

City of Austin, District Demographics and Maps. Accessed March 25, 2018. Available at http://www.austintexas.gov//page/district-demographics.

———. Environmental Commission. Accessed October 4, 2017. Available at https:// austintexas.gov/envboard.

———. Imagine Austin. Accessed May 10, 2018. Available at https://www.austintexas .gov/imagineaustin.

———. "Memorandum: Assessment of Fiscal Impact for Charter Amendments." August 29, 2012.

———. Office of the City Clerk. Election History. Accessed April 19–21, 2018; May 8–10, 2018; May 25, 2018; November 29, 2018. Available at http://www.ci.austin.tx.us /election/search.cfm.

———. Office of the City Manager. Accessed May 27, 2018. Available at https://www .austintexas.gov/department/city-manager.

———. Ordinance No. 20120802-015, August 2, 2012. Accessed June 2, 2018. Available at http://www.austintexas.gov/edims/document.cfm?id=174695.

———. Ordinance No. 20150129-026, January 29, 2015. Accessed June 2, 2018. Available at http://www.austintexas.gov/edims/document.cfm?id=225685.

———. Proposition 3 Results: The 10–1 Plan, November 6, 2012. Accessed May 12, 2018; June 3, 2018. Available at http://www.austintexas.gov/sites/default/files/files/Planning /Demographics/Prop_3_2012.pdf.

Clark, Alistair, and Timothy B. Krebs. "Elections and Policy Responsiveness." In *Oxford Handbook of Urban Politics,* edited by Karen Mossberger, Susan E. Clarke, and Peter John. New York: Oxford University Press, 2012.

Coppola, Sarah. "Austin Voters Rejected City Council Districts Six Times in the Past. Will This Year Be Different?" *Austin American-Statesman,* September 15, 2012. Available at https://www.statesman.com/news/local/austin-voters-rejected-city-council -districts-six-times-the-past-will-this-year-different/koR4lTOGOpzbeRKrBbCCPM/.

——. "City Offers Residents 2 District Scenarios." *Austin American-Statesman*, June 30, 2012. A1, A11.

——. "Observers: Door-to-Door Effort Fueled Prop. 3 Win." *Austin American-Statesman*, November 8, 2012. A1, A4.

——. "Pros and Cons of Council Districts." *Austin American-Statesman*, September 24, 2012.

"Council's Attempt at New Voting Districts Misses the Point." *Austin American-Statesman*, April 8, 2002. A14. Editorial.

Dunbar, Wells. "David Van Os on Single-Member Districts." *Austin Chronicle*, February 28, 2008. Available at http://www.austinchronicle.com/daily/news/2008-02-28/597508.

——. "The Single-Member Situation: Movement Afoot—Once Again—to Ask Voters to Approve City Council Districts." *Austin Chronicle*, February 25, 2011. Available at https://www.austinchronicle.com/news/2011-02-25/the-single-member-situation/.

Engstrom, Richard L., and Richard N. Engstrom. "The Majority Vote Rule and Runoff Primaries in the United States." *Electoral Studies* 27, no. 3 (September 2008): 407–416.

Engstrom, Richard L., and Michael D. McDonald. "The Election of Blacks to City Councils: Clarifying the Impact of Electoral Arrangements on the Seats/Population Relationship." *American Political Science Review* 75, no. 2 (1981): 344–354.

Eulau, Heinz, and Kenneth Prewitt. *Labyrinths of Democracy: Adaptations, Linkages, Representation, and Policies in Urban Politics*. Indianapolis: Bobbs-Merrill, 1973.

Findell, Elizabeth. "Austin City Manager Will Replace Executive Team after Open Recruitment." *Austin American-Statesman*, July 27, 2018. Available at https://www.statesman.com/news/local/austin-city-manager-will-replace-executive-team-after-open-recruitment/k4vm8xqD9hiGq5N3w2axHN/.

——. "Jimmy Flannigan, Alison Alter Bring Sophomore Shift to City Council." *Austin American-Statesman*, June 11, 2018. Available at https://www.mystatesman.com/news/local-govt--politics/jimmy-flannigan-alison-alter-bring-sophomore-shift-city-council/Sx5VnG2riEQsPVtX9R3ohI/.

Florida, Richard. *Cities and the Creative Class*. New York: Routledge, 2005.

——. "More Losers Than Winners in America's New Economic Geography." *CityLab*, January 30, 2013. Available at http://www.citylab.com/work/2013/01/more-losers-winners-americas-new-economic-geography/4465/.

——. *The New Urban Crisis*. New York: Basic Books, 2017.

——. *The Rise of the Creative Class: And How It's Transforming Work, Leisure, Community and Everyday Life*. New York: Basic Books, 2002.

——. *The Rise of the Creative Class—Revisited: 10th Anniversary Edition—Revised and Expanded*. New York: Basic Books, 2014.

Gierzynski, Anthony, and David Breaux. "Money and Votes in State Legislative Elections." *Legislative Studies Quarterly* 16, no. 2 (1991): 203–217.

Grodach, Carl. "Before and after the Creative City: The Politics of Urban Cultural Policy in Austin, Texas." *Journal of Urban Affairs* 34, no. 1 (2012): 81–97.

Grumet, Bridget. "Poll Shows How We're Split over CodeNEXT and What Issue Can Bring Us Together." *Austin American-Statesman*, May 11, 2018. Available at http://viewpoints.blog.mystatesman.com/2018/05/11/poll-shows-how-were-split-over-codenext-and-what-issue-can-bring-us-together/.

Haag, Stefan. "Voter Turnout and Representation in the Austin City Council Elections, 2014." Austin Community College Center for Public Policy and Political Studies, November 2015.

Haag, Stefan, Jeff Smith, and William R. "Peck" Young. "Studies of Political Statistics: Voter Turnout in Two Austin City Council Districts: 2014 and 2016." Austin Community College Center for Public Policy and Political Studies, March 2017.

Hajnal, Zoltan L. *America's Uneven Democracy: Race, Turnout, and Representation in City Politics.* New York: Cambridge University Press, 2010.

Hajnal, Zoltan, and Jessica Trounstine. "Where Turnout Matters: The Consequences of Uneven Turnout in City Politics." *Journal of Politics* 67, no. 2 (2005): 515–535.

Hall, Michael. "The City of the Eternal Boom." *Texas Monthly*, March 2016.

Hasan, Syeda. "Council Votes Unanimously to Scrap CodeNEXT." *Austin Monitor,* August 10, 2018. Available at https://www.austinmonitor.com/stories/2018/08/city -council-votes-unanimously-to-scrap-codenext/.

Heilig, Peggy, and Robert J. Mundt. *Your Voice at City Hall: The Politics, Procedures and Policies of District Representation.* Albany: State University of New York Press, 1984.

Hernandez, Nina. "Rebooted City Council Gets a New Chance to Fix Austin," *Austin Chronicle,* January 11, 2019. Available at https://www.austinchronicle.com/news /2019-01-11/rebooted-city-council-gets-a-new-chance-to-fix-austin/.

Herrera, Sebastian. "A Year into Amazon's Much-Hyped HQ2 Search, Austin—and the Other Finalists—Are Still Waiting." *512 Tech by Austin American-Statesman*, September 4, 2018. Available at https://www.512tech.com/technology/year-into-amazon -much-hyped-hq2-search-austin-and-the-other-finalists-are-still-waiting/iMLYo8 igcVQEEHb3S7TlRJ/?utm_source=newspaper&utm_medium=email&utm _campaign=5736906&ecmp=newspaper_email&.

Hicks, Nolan. "Austin City Manager Marc Ott Leaving for Washington Job." *Austin American-Statesman*, August 12, 2016. Available at https://www.mystatesman.com /news/local/austin-city-manager-marc-ott-leaving-for-washington-job/9TY6M G22oRQIiCECiNY9cI/.

———. "Austin Council Gives City Manager Marc Ott a $22,000 Raise." *Austin American-Statesman*, June 14, 2016. Available at https://www.mystatesman.com/news/local -govt--politics/austin-council-gives-city-manager-marc-ott-000-raise/CMiFR V4CJXLvGC9JImG1RK/.

Hicks, Nolan, and Elizabeth Findell. "What Will Addition of Alter, Flannigan Bring to Austin City Council?" *Austin American-Statesman*, January 15, 2016. Available at https://www.mystatesman.com/news/local/how-did-each-austin-city-council -member-perform-2015/cjRONuhnZQOzm2s9WdcwKN/.

Holman, Mirya R. *Women in Politics in the American City.* Philadelphia: Temple University Press, 2015.

Humphrey, David C. *Austin: A History of the Capital City.* Austin: Texas State Historical Association, 1997.

Independent Citizens Redistricting Commission of Austin, Texas. Final Report. October 24, 2014.

Jacobson, Gary C. "The Effects of Campaign Spending in Congressional Elections." *American Political Science Review* 72, no. 2 (1978): 469–491.

Jankowski, Philip. "Did Backers of City Audit Proposition Skirt 'Dark Money' Restrictions?," *Austin American-Statesman*, September 25, 2018. Available at https://www

.statesman.com/news/20180918/did-backers-of-city-audit-proposition-skirt-dark
-money-restrictions.

———. "For Good or Bad, Petition Elections a Growing Trend in Texas." *Austin American-Statesman*, January 24, 2019. Available at https://www.statesman.com/news
/20190124/for-good-or-bad-petition-elections-growing-trend-in-texas.

———. "Petition Filed to Require an Efficiency Audit of Austin City Hall." *Austin American-Statesman*, July 13, 2018. Available at https://www.statesman.com/news
/local/petition-filed-require-efficiency-audit-austin-cityhall/t7CqUKaXqWF3UD
go7vblnM/.

Judd, Dennis R., and Todd Swanstrom. *City Politics: The Political Economy of Urban America*. New York: Pearson, 2006.

Kaleem, Jaweed. "'Freedom City'? Going beyond 'Sanctuary,' Austin, Texas, Vows to Curtail Arrests." *Los Angeles Times*, June 19, 2018. Available at http://www.latimes
.com/nation/la-na-austin-freedom-city-2018-story.html.

Karnig, Albert K. "Black Representation on City Councils: The Impact of District Elections and Socioeconomic Factors." *Urban Affairs Quarterly* 12, no. 2 (1976): 223–242.

Katz, Bruce. "Envisioning the New Localism." *Public Management* 100, no. 1 (2018): 6–9.

Kaufmann, Karen M. *The Urban Voter: Group Conflict and Mayoral Voting Behavior in American Cities*. Ann Arbor: University of Michigan Press, 2004.

Kerr, Jeffrey Stuart. *Seat of Empire: The Embattled Birth of Austin, Texas*. Lubbock: Texas Tech University Press, 2013.

King, Michael. "Cronk to Reorganize Management Team." *Austin Chronicle*, August, 3, 2018. Available at https://www.austinchronicle.com/news/2018-08-03/cronk-to
-reorganize-management-team/.

———. "Point Austin: Strange Bedfellows, Stranger Politics." *Austin Chronicle*, August 10, 2018. Available at https://www.austinchronicle.com/news/2018-08-10/point
-austin-strange-bedfellows-stranger-politics/.

———. "Point Austin: What You Say, and How You Say It." *Austin Chronicle*, August 17, 2018. Available at https://www.austinchronicle.com/news/2018-08-17/point-austin
-what-you-say-and-how-you-say-it/.

Kirkland, Patricia A. "Social Class and Representation in American Cities." Working paper, August 25, 2018.

Kotkin, Joel. "Richard Florida Concedes the Limits of the Creative Class." *Daily Beast*, March 20, 2013. Available at http://www.thedailybeast.com/articles/2013/03/20
/richard-florida-concedes-the-limits-of-the-creative-class.html.

Krebs, Timothy B. "Political Experience and Fundraising in City Council Elections." *Social Science Quarterly* 82, no. 3 (2001): 536–551.

Lewis, Paul G., and Max Neiman. *Custodians of Place: Governing the Growth and Development of Cities*. Washington, DC: Georgetown University Press, 2009.

Lim, Andra. "How Did Each Austin City Council Member Perform in 2015." *Austin American-Statesman*, January 15, 2016. Available at https://www.statesman.com
/news/20160904/how-did-each-austin-city-council-member-perform-in-2015.

Lisheron, Mark. "Austin City Council Goes Heavy on Affordable Housing in a Major Bond Issue." *Texas Monitor*, July 2, 2018. Available at https://texasmonitor.org/austin
-city-concil-goes-heavy-on-affordable-housing-in-a-major-bond-issue/.

Long, Joshua. *Weird City: Sense of Place and Creative Resistance in Austin, Texas*. Austin: University of Texas Press, 2010.

MacCorkle, Stuart A. *Austin's Three Forms of Government*. San Antonio: Naylor, 1973.

MacManus, Susan A. "City Council Election Procedures and Minority Representation: Are They Related?" *Social Science Quarterly* 59, no. 1 (1978): 153–161.

Martin, Ken. "8–2–1 Plan Near-Certain to Go on Ballot." *Austin Bulldog*, July 31, 2012. Available at https://www.theaustinbulldog.org/index.php?option=com_content& view=article&id=208:8-2-1-plan-certain-to-go-on-ballot&catid=3:main-articles.

———. "10–1 Elections Cost $6.3 Million: Political Action Committees Laid Out $726,000 for Independent Expenditures to Influence Voters." *Austin Bulldog*, March 27, 2015. Available at https://www.theaustinbulldog.org/index.php?option=com_content& view=article&id=342:10-1-elections-cost-63-million&catid=3:main-articles.

———. "Council's Ballot Language Triggers Lawsuit(s)." *Austin Bulldog*, August 11, 2018. Available at https://www.theaustinbulldog.org/index.php?option=com_content&v iew=article&id=430:councils-ballot-language-triggers-lawsuits&catid=3:main -articles.

———. "An Economically Diverse City Council: City No Longer Governed Only by Very Well-to-Do Citizens." *Austin Bulldog*, June 15, 2015. Available at https://www.the austinbulldog.org/index.php?option=com_content&view=article&id=354%3Aan -economically-diverse-city-council&catid=3%3Amain-articles&Itemid=15.

———. "Maps Prove a Select Few Govern Austin: Forty Years of Election History Expose Extent of Disparities." *Austin Bulldog*, August 4, 2011. Available at https://www .theaustinbulldog.org/index.php?option=com_content&view=article&id=150:at -large-elections-favor-anglo-choices&catid=3:main-articles#comment-213.

Molotch, Harvey. "The City as a Growth Machine: Toward a Political Economy of Place." *American Journal of Sociology* 82, no. 2 (1976): 309–332.

Neely, Christopher. "Austin City Council Officially Slashes Its Committee Structure." *Community Impact*, February 16, 2017. Available at https://communityimpact.com /austin/city-county/2017/02/16/austin-city-council-officially-slashes-committee -structure/.

Nold, Susan, and Christopher Kennedy. "It's Up to the People of Austin to Make Mean-ingful Change out of the '10–1' System." *UT News*, November 17, 2015. Available at https://news.utexas.edu/2015/11/17/making-meaningful-change-out-of-the-10-1 -system.

Olson, David M. *Nonpartisan Elections: A Case Analysis*. Austin: University of Texas Press, 1965.

Orum, Anthony M. *Power, Money and People: The Making of Modern Austin*. Austin: Texas Monthly Press, 1987.

Pagano, Elizabeth. "The More (Maps) the Merrier! A Brief Introduction to the ICRC's Proposed City Council District Map—and a Few Alternatives." *Austin Chronicle*, October 25, 2013. Available at https://www.austinchronicle.com/news/2013-10-25 /the-more-maps-the-merrier/.

———. "New Council Plans to Change Meetings, Committees." KUT, January 9, 2015. Avail-able at http://www.kut.org/post/new-council-plans-change-meetings-committees.

Pagano, Michael A., and Ann O'M. Bowman. *Cityscapes and Capital: The Politics of Urban Development*. Baltimore, MD: Johns Hopkins University Press, 1995.

Partin, Randall W. "Assessing the Impact of Campaign Spending in Governors' Races." *Political Research Quarterly* 55, no. 1 (2002): 213–233.

Peck, Jamie. "Struggling with the Creative Class," *International Journal of Urban and Regional Research* 29, no. 4 (2005): 740–770.

Pitkin, Hanna F. *The Concept of Representation*. Berkeley: University of California Press, 1967.

Polinard, J. L., Robert D. Wrinkle, Tomas Longoria, and Norman E. Binder. *Electoral Structure and Urban Policy: The Impact on Mexican American Communities*. Armonk, NY: M. E. Sharpe, 1994.

Reinhold, Robert. "Booming Austin Fears It Will Lose Its Charms." *New York Times*, October 8, 1983. Available at https://www.nytimes.com/1983/10/08/us/booming -austin-fears-it-will-lose-its-charms.html.

Rescorla, Bob, Molly Hults, and Rusty Heckaman. "Brief Overview of the City of Austin's Government Structure Establishment and Evolution." In *City of Austin Resource Guide, 4*, Austin History Center, 2017.

Rice, Bradley Robert. "Commission Form of City Government." Austin: Texas State Historical Association. Accessed February 11, 2018. Available at https://tshaonline .org/handbook/online/articles/moc01.

———. *Progressive Cities: The Commission Government Movement in America, 1901– 1920*. Austin: University of Texas Press, 1977.

Robinson, Theodore P., and Thomas R. Dye. "Reformism and Black Representation on City Councils." *Social Science Quarterly* 59, no. 1 (1978): 133–141.

Rockwell, Lilly. "As Women Take Majority on Austin City Council, Staff Warned to Expect More Questions, Longer Talks," *Austin American-Statesman*, May 15, 2015. Available at http://cityhall.blog.statesman.com/2015/05/12/as-women-take-majority -on-austin-city-council-staff-warned-to-expect-more-questions-longer-talks/.

———. "Austin City Council and Mayor Approve Plan for More Staff," *Austin American- Statesman*, September 24, 2016. Available at https://statesman.com/NEWS/20160924 /Austin-City-Council-and-mayor-approve-plan-for-more-staff.

———. "Austin City Council Staffing Plan Grows, but Not as Mayor Had Hoped." *Austin American-Statesman*, March 31, 2015. Available at https://www.mystatesman.com /news/local/austin-city-council-staffing-plan-grows-but-not-mayor-had-hoped/UG XKvnz8FsoBmCx9IOnu7J/.

———. "Austin Council Members Fuming about City-Led Training Session on Women." *Austin American-Statesman*, May 13, 2015. Available at https://www.mystatesman .com/news/local/austin-council-members-fuming-about-city-led-training-session -women/fIURkxmCimnsSAY1GEj5DN/.

———. "What Do Austin Residents Think of the City Council?" *Austin American- Statesman*, January 16, 2016. Available at http://cityhall.blog.statesman.com/2016 /01/15/what-do-austin-residents-think-of-the-city-council/.

———. "What Will New Republican Members Bring to Austin City Council?" *Austin American-Statesman*, December 17, 2014. Available at https://www.mystatesman .com/news/what-will-new-republican-members-bring-austin-city-council/Q3Su 8Z7eudklhYzDp7HvEK/.

Rosenblatt, Josh. "Citizens Group Sees African-American Plurality in 10–1 Districting Plan." *Austin Monitor*, July 9, 2012. Available at https://www.austinmonitor.com /stories/2012/07/citizens-group-sees-african-american-plurality-in-10-1-districting -plan/.

———. "Geopolitical Fault Lines: Austin's Latest Attempt at Single-Member Districts Is Getting a Mixed Response." *Austin Chronicle*, July 6, 2012. Available at https://www.austinchronicle.com/news/2012-07-06/Geopolitical-Fault-Lines/.

Seabrook, Nicholas R. "Money and State Legislative Elections: The Conditional Impact of Political Context." *American Politics Research* 38, no. 3 (2010): 399–424.

Solomon, Dan. "The Texas Lege's Culture War on Austin Has Come to a Cuddly Cease-fire." *Texas Monthly*, March 20, 2019. Available at https://www.texasmonthly.com/politics/texas-legislature-cuddly-ceasefire/.

Staniszewski, Frank. "Ideology and Practice in Municipal Government Reform: A Case Study of Austin," *Studies in Politics*, series 1, paper no. 8, 20–21. Austin: University of Texas Press, 1977.

Stone, Harold A., Don K. Price, and Kathryn H. Stone. *City Manager Government in Nine Cities*. Chicago: Public Administration Service, 1940.

Svara, James H. *Two Decades of Continuity and Change in American City Councils*. Washington, DC: National League of Cities, 2003.

Swearingen, William Scott, Jr. *Environmental City: People, Place, Politics, and the Meaning of Modern Austin*. Austin: University of Texas Press, 2010.

Tausanovitch, Chris, and Christopher Warshaw. "Measuring Constituent Policy Preferences in Congress, State Legislatures, and Cities." *Journal of Politics* 75, no. 2 (2013): 330–342.

———. "Representation in Municipal Government." *American Political Science Review* 108, no. 3 (2014): 605–641.

Travis County Clerk, City of Austin Election Results. Accessed May 8, 2019. Available at http://traviselectionresults.com/enr/results/display.do;jsessionid=96ecb67cc9c79f688c96c537a7d0?criteria.electionId=20181106&formSubmitted=1.

Tretter, Eliot M. *Shadows of a Sunbelt City: The Environment, Racism, and the Knowledge Economy in Austin*. Athens: University of Georgia Press, 2015.

Trounstine, Jessica. *Political Monopolies in American Cities: The Rise and Fall of Bosses and Reformers*. Chicago: University of Chicago Press, 2008.

———. "Representation and Accountability in Cities," *Annual Review of Political Science* 13 (2010): 407–423.

Trounstine, Jessica, and Melody E. Valdini. "The Context Matters: The Effects of Single-Member versus At-Large Districts on City Council Diversity." *American Journal of Political Science* 52, no. 3 (2008): 554–569.

Unforeseen, The. Directed by Laura Dunn. New York: Cinetic, 2007.

U.S. Census Bureau, "Annual Estimates of the Resident Population for Incorporated Places of 50,000 or More, Ranked by July 1, 2017 Population," American Fact Finder, May 2018. Available at https://factfinder.census.gov/faces/tableservices/jsf/pages/productview.xhtml?src=bkmk.

———. "Census Bureau Reveals Fastest-Growing Large Cities," May 24, 2018. Available at https://census.gov/newsroom/press-releases/2018/estimates-cities.html#table.

"VoteTracker." *Austin American-Statesman*. Accessed April 9–20, 2018. Available at https://apps.statesman.com/votetracker/entities/austin-city-council/.

"Way to Better Representation, A." *Austin American-Statesman*, January 22, 2000. A14. Editorial.

Welch, Susan, and Timothy Bledsoe. *Urban Reform and Its Consequences: A Study in Representation*. Chicago: University of Chicago Press, 1988.

Zandan, Peter. "The Zandan Poll: Voices of the Austin Community: 2015 Poll Results." Accessed February 1, 2018. Available at https://austinsurvey.files.wordpress.com /2015/03/zandan-poll-2015-voices-of-the-austin-community-c2ad-results.pdf.

———. "The Zandan Poll: Voices of the Austin Community: 2017 Poll Results." Accessed February 1, 2018. Available at https://austinsurvey.files.wordpress.com/2017/04 /zandanpoll2017_topline-final.pdf.

Zaragoza, Sandra. "Q&A: Creative Class Author on Austin." *Austin Business Journal*, November 22, 2010. Available at https://www.bizjournals.com/austin/blog/creative /2010/11/qa-creative-class-author-on-austin.html.

Voter turnout, 19, 22, 26, 33–34, 36–37, 47–48
Voting Rights Act, 16, 31–33, 48

Wards, 14–15; in Austin, 20–23
Warshaw, Christopher, 12, 54
Welch, Susan, 18, 55, 59–60, 62
Wentworth, Jeff, 38–39
West Austin, 10, 37, 44, 50, 58

White, Ben, 24
Williamson County, 10
Women on the City Council, 58–59, 65
Wooldridge, A. P., 23

Zilker, Andrew, 20–21, 23–24, 85n42
Zimmermann, Don, 71–72
Zoning and Platting Commission, 78

Ann O'M. Bowman is a Professor of Government in the Department of Public Service and Administration in the Bush School of Government and Public Service at Texas A&M University and holds the Hazel Davis and Robert Kennedy Endowed Chair. She is the co-author of several books including *State and Local Government* and *Terra Incognita: Vacant Land and Urban Strategies.*